谨以此书献给
60年来为中国西藏发展做出努力的人们

This book is dedicated to
those who have contributed to the development of China's Tibet over the past 60 years.

尹集钧，美籍华人。1927年生于四川，1980年到美国。

20世纪80年代，尹集钧在美国华文报章发表多篇评论，出版有《南京大屠杀》（1995年美国出版，中英文双语），《1937，南京大救援》（1997年香港出版，中文），*The Angels of Nanking*（中国香港出版，英文），《细菌战大屠杀》（2001年美国出版，中英文双语）。

从1952年起，尹集钧先后八次前往西藏，拍摄并记录了许多珍贵的影像与文字。2001年，尹集钧专心投入西藏专题研究，他用了十几年的时间将零碎的素材和几百篇诗文整合编写成《虔诚如诗》和《昭心若歌》，并在美国出版发行。《虔诚如诗》出版后，世界看到了“西藏在物质建设方面”的进步。国务院新闻办公室购买了三千本，送呈中国驻外机构，新闻办还向海外推荐了该书。《昭心若歌》将《虔诚如诗》里没有展开的细节充分展开，展现中央政府对西藏人民信仰的尊重与保护，进一步反映汉藏人民亲如一家、共享社会建设成果的历史风貌。

Mr. James Yin, the author, was born in Sichuan, China in 1927. He came to the USA in 1980.

In 1980s, he frequently made comments in Chinese newspapers, and in 1995 he published *Rape of Nanking* (in Chinese and English) in the USA. In 1997 he pulished *1937, Salvage of Nanking* (in Chinese) and *The Angels of Nanking* (in English) in HK. In 2001 he published *The Rape of Biological Warfare* (in Chinese and English) in the USA.

Since his first trip to Tibet in 1952, he went to Tibet eight times and documented a lot of precious photos and facts in Tibet. In 2001 he devoted himself to the study and research of Tibet ever since. He integrated fragmentary materials and hundreds of poems and essays over ten years and finally produced the book *Poetic Devoutness* and *Spiritual Heart Song* which was published in USA. After the publication of *Poetic Devoutness*, The world saw Tibet's progress in material development. The State Council Information Office purchased 3,000 books at that time and sent them to Chinese agencies abroad. The office also recommended the book to overseas. The book *Spiritual Heart Song* displays more details which are not fully developed in *Poetic Devoutness*, showing respect and protection for the beliefs of the Tibetan people, and further reflecting the history that the Han and Tibetan people share the prosperity of social construction as one family.

The Past and Present : 60 Years of Tibet in My Eyes

雪域圣地的前世今生：我眼中的西藏60年

［美］尹集钧 / 编著　朱永敏　秦　丹　尹家琤 / 译

Author James Yin

Translator Zhu Yongmin / Qin Dan / Yin Jiacheng

天地出版社
TIANDI PRESS

序言

在西方世界，人们一提及西藏，不可能不被各自所持有的政治利益和意识形态所左右，于是西藏的真实显得云遮雾罩。

然而，西藏的真实是存在的。西藏从20世纪20年代十三世达赖喇嘛进行初阶段的20年改革尝试，到20世纪60年代开始的大规模改革开放，已使延续了多个世纪完全封闭停滞落后的雪域，变成了一个完全开放的弃旧拓新的天地。

这些变化，不是哪一个人物的恩赐，不是哪一个神王的法力所致，而是全体在藏的人民大众冷眉面对少数人发动的利益纠缠，热诚笑对极端恶劣气候的蹂躏所获得的一点求新图变和社会进步。

这点进步，在西藏历史上是快的，在当前世界情势下是慢的。说快，是指她用了不到一个世纪（从十三世达赖喇嘛1913年的新政算起）或半个世纪（从十四世达赖喇嘛出亡印度的1959年算起）完成了西方用好几个世纪才完成的由农奴经济到市场经济的过渡。

今天，西藏的价值，已不仅仅关于中国至高无上的主权，更无关西方情思厚重的“香格里拉”的情结，而是戈尔所警告的那样，关系到人类整个文明能否免于自然灾害从而得到延续的大题。

世界的政治家，世界的媒体人，世界的学者们：

请为西藏人民大众过去的努力，给一点鼓励的微笑吧！

请为西藏社会更多一点的和平和安定，给西藏人民更多一点的祝福吧！

本书呈现了西藏一个世纪以来的组照，组照依同一背景或同一焦点或同一主题进行真实的对比。这些照片，没有红与黑，没有独尊和傲慢，只是向世界诉说西藏变革的艰苦和辛酸，以及西藏民众的悲悯和无悔。

西藏，比起西方来说还很落后，但正是这一质朴的小小群体，还在为全球苦苦守护着一大片碧水蓝天。

杰克·麦克劳林 博士（美国，教育家）
玛丽·艾莉丝·蕾丝芭 教授（美国，社会活动家）

FOREWORD

Whenever people in the West mention Tibet, politics and ideology issues blot out in all directions like a huge avalanche that submerges the entire truth of Tibet.

Nonetheless, the Tibet does exist. For the Tibet an modernization, from the 1920s when 13th Dalai Lama set out to reform attempt was 20 years, and from the 1960s when started the large-scale open reform, has 50 years, which had turned Tibet from centuries of a tightly closed, stagnated, and backward snow-covered territory into a completely open, new, and developed field.

These changes were not brought forth by the grace of one legendary man, nor by one God, but by each and every people who has lived through the devastation of political and ideological entanglements, as well as the hardship of extreme harsh weather conditions.

The progress, if measured by the history of Tibet, was a rapid move, however, compared to the current global circumstances, was a slow process. Claiming it a rapid move, I refer it to the time span of less than a century (from 1913, 13th Dalai Lama) or the time span less than a half century (from 1959), for Tibet to complete what the Western world took several hundreds of years, making transition from the agricultural slavery economy to market economy.

Today, Tibet's value exceeds the Chinese sovereignty supreme, the Western's goodwill-"Shangrila", and no doubt its value if far more holy than the prayers of Lama Monarchy in preserving lives. Al Gore has been warning us: This is great concern whether human culture can survive the natural disaster, Tibet's value is critically related to the human survival.

My world-acclaimed statesmen, media faculty and scholars:
Please give encouraging smile and a little more wish, for all the people of Tibet, and the efforts they have made in the past.

Presented here, are groups photos of Tibet for a century. Each set of photos, taken in different times, was paired either identical background, identical focal points, or identical subjects. They do not have the Red Flag nor the Snow Lion Flag, and no ideology. Just return to the original truth, and empathize with the Tibet's masses and their endurance and mercy.

Compared to the West, Tibet still has a long way to complete her ideal. This backward small community is not only dealing with their own basic emotional needs but also protecting a plateau of blue water and azure sky for the world.

Dr. Jack McLaughlin (Educator USA)
Prof. Mary Alice Rathbun (Social Activist. USA)

CONTENTS 目　录

CONTENTS
目录

第一章 不悔的拉萨之恋

Chapter 1 Unregretful Love for Lhasa

天上的街市

回廊漫步

圣城惊览

地标云翩

Heavenly Market

Strolling in the Barkhor Street

Views of the Sacred City

The Cloud Leads to the Landmark

三座金塔 巴郭噶林 2007年 The three Golden Pagodas, Pargo Kaling in 2007.

蓝天下有三座金塔的地方，那就是梦里的拉萨
（出自雪域民歌）

Under the blue sky stand three Golden Pagodas, Lhasa in the dream
(from Snowland songs)

赤脚行路的底层妇女 1900年左右

Women from underclass walking barefoot around 1900.

天寒，裸脚，衣单，
山蒙，沙飞，风乱。
朝圣途苦远，
步步艰难有谁怜。

Cold winter, bare-footed and thinly clothed,
Misty mountains, flying sand and violent storms.
The pilgrim journeys far and hard,
Who took pity on the hardships.

苍天，碧空，云卷，
地舒，人寰，日暖。
路牌指拉萨，
铁桥哈达正召唤。

Heavens, skies and clouds,
Comforting ground, the world, and warm sunshine.
The road sign pointing to Lhasa,
Iron bridges and ha da calling.

三座金塔

三座金色的佛塔（巴郭噶林）建于1645年，即清顺治二年。它们位于药王山和布达拉山之间的山口，是通往拉萨的大门。佛塔被称为“神变塔”，以此纪念释迦牟尼以多种神通打败外敌，保卫拉萨。一塔守城，一塔镇宫，一塔护民。

巴郭噶林 1938年 Pargo Kaling in 1938.

圣书《马翁郎登》早已警告过：“欧洲人将会入侵和征服……”真是不幸言中。1904年8月，英国军队就是经过这些佛塔攻占了拉萨。

英国人在这次入侵里掠夺多少财宝，没有公开的记录，只知英军指挥官荣赫鹏用了400头驴子运送他掠获的西藏古宝到达印度，这些古宝现分存于欧洲的一些博物馆。

Pargo Kaling

Three Golden Pagodas were built in 1645, the second year of Emperor Shunzi of the Qing Dynasty. Located at the pass between the Chakpori and Marpori, the three Buddha pagodas are the gateway to Lhasa. Called "Pagodas of God's Magic", the Pagodas were meant to commemorate Sakyamuni's magic powers to defeat the external enemies and protect Lhasa. One for defending Lhasa, one for governing Potala and one for protecting the people.

The sacred book *Maong Lungten* warned earlier: "The Europeans will invade and conquer..." It did happen unfortunately. In August 1904, the British armies invaded Lhasa by passing these pagodas.

There are no public records as to how much the British looted during the invasion. What is known is that the British commander Francis Younghusband bragged using 400 donkeys to carry his collection of Tibetan treasures to India. Those ancient treasure articles are now kept in some museums in Europe.

三座金塔，在布达拉宫坐落的红山西南，是拉萨的大门。

白色塔身，金色塔顶，闪耀在阳光下。

而三座金塔光泽的亮与暗，在历代观察家眼里，已成为拉萨地方政权统治盛与衰的标志。

这是因为塔上的金色会褪，需要增补。

白石常被鸟类粪便堆污变黑，

需要时常加以清除。

There are three golden pagodas at the southwest part of the Marpori where Potala Palace stands. They are the main entrance to Lhasa. The pagodas have white towers and golden caps, shining in sunshine. In the eyes of observers of all ages, the lightness and darkness of the three pagodas are a sign of prosperity and decline of the local power in Lhasa. This is because the golden color on top can fade away and needs repaint, while the white stone pagoda can be dirtied by bird droppings and needs regular cleaning.

英军攻入拉萨 1904年 British troops attacking Lhasa in 1904.

英国大兵，挥师进拉萨，
千年雪，第一杀。
无精打采落魄过佛塔，
林枯了，丘成沙。

The British soldiers marching into Lhasa,
First slay in a thousand years.
Passing the Buddhist pagoda spiritlessly,
The forests depleted into sand domes.

2007年布达拉宫下的巴郭噶林

Pargo Kaling under Potala Palace in 2007.

年年新事除旧事，
人笑车驰香巴拉*。
香巴拉就在你心上，
香巴拉就在这拉萨。

Discarding the old year for the new,
Driving smilingly through Shambala.*
In your heart is Shambala,
Right in Lhasa is Shambala.

---

*香巴拉：又译为“香格里拉”，理想的佛教圣地。

*Shambala: aka Shagrila, the ideal sacred site for spreading Buddhism.

放眼望远皆是沙，
沙山沙岭令人怕。
大漠荒原垃圾地，
不是拉萨是垃撒。

Taking a broad view ahead,
I saw on hills and ground sands spread.
Lhasa was not found alright,
Only desert was in my sight.

巴郭噶林 1938年 Pargo Kaling in 1938.

黄荒景一片，
生机全未见。
官贵策大马，
神宫仍漠然。

On the bleak hillside,
Vitality was not there.
But high officials were still on big horses,
And dignitaries still enjoyed themselves no matter where.

巴郭噶林与布达拉宫 2015年 Pargo Kaling and Potala Palace in 2015.

神塔洁玉如藏心，
顶天立地似藏人。
天人合一乃我祈，
一片赤诚拜天庭。

The holy pagodas are clean as the Tibetan heart,
Stand indomitably as the Tibetan stand.
Unity of heaven and men is what I pray for,
With pure piety I worship heaven so grand.

三座神塔洁如玉，
金顶冲天指向云。
塔神回归蓝天笑，
布宫楼外分外明。

The three pagodas are clean as white marbles,
Their golden caps point to the white cloud.
The deity returns and the blue sky smiles,
Harmony returns and people are proud.

金塔粪成堆，	*Stained by bird droppings,*
任由风雨摧，	*To wind and rain the white pagoda exposed.*
神王自身也不保，	*Theocracy could not protect himself,*
问谁?	*Whom to ask? You supposed.*
行人衣衫破，	*The passerby had worn-out clothes,*
童儿脸颜灰，	*Children had pale faces.*
都成天下沦落人，	*Where to find a happy life,*
怨谁?	*Where were those places?*

巴郭噶林遥对药王山 1938年

Pargo Kaling and Chakpori in 1938.

塔神哪能变像，	*Having different expressions in half of the century,*
半个世纪两个样。	*The holy pagodas have changed its appearance.*
有人白宫美元梦，	*Dreaming of dollars,*
呓断神塔早倒塌。	*Someone hoped for the pagoda's fall and disappearance.*
几曾塌，	*Yet having not fallen,*
却是换颜金顶闪。	*They have their golden caps shining.*
引人磕头，	*Attracting pilgrims' coming,*
引人跪下，	*Attracting people's kowtowing,*
虔诚一枝花。	*Being devoutness as a flower.*

同一个天，不同晴与暗，
恰似轮回在转。
同一座塔，不同色与颜，
莫非你我涂演。

The same sky, but with varying brightness and darkness,
Like a spinning wheel.
The same pagoda, but in different colors,
It might be true that you and I painted it.

远眺巴郭噶林和药王山 2004年
Overlooking Pargo Kaling and Chakpori in 2004.

金塔影照一百年，
半百保守半惊变。
惊，
惊了个眼花缭乱。
变，
变了个地覆天翻。
有人喜，有人叹，
有人鼓掌，
有人骂天。
莫急躁，处坦然，
是非自在众人心，
史书总归后人撰。

The pictures of Golden Pagodas of a hundred years,
Half a century of conservative, and half a century of shocking changes.
Shocks,
Dazzling the eyes.
Changes,
Shaking the earth and the sky.
Some happy, and some sad,
Some applauding,
Some cursing.
No haste,
And be calm, in the hearts of people lies the truth,
By future generations history is written.

帐篷前的乞丐 1938年

A beggar standing before his tent in 1938.

拉萨的街道 2007年

Lhasa's street in 2007.

圣城拉萨回头看，
一街跪乞号天，
一眼依墙避寒。
枯手捂苦难诉，
风撕破衣烂衫。

Looking back at the Holy city of Lhasa,
On the streets beggars on their knees,
Against the walls to keep warm.
Where to vent grievance?
In the wind thinly clad in rags.

圣城拉萨在今天，
一城梵烟弥漫，
一歌悄飘雪原。
弯弯曲水悠去，
满廊访客流连。

In today's Holy city of Lhasa,
Filled with smoke from Buddhist,
Songs heard over the snowland.
Winding streams flowing,
Pavilions full of visitors.

两个拉萨不同画，
两重风景两重缘。

Different pictures of two Lhasa,
Two scenes of two destinies.

城中城

拉萨圣中圣，
城中又有城。
千万乞求凄厉声，
撕破雪域一净景。

20世纪50年代初拉萨贫民窟——“邦”村的乞丐群

A City Within a City

Lhasa, the Holiest of the Holy,
A city within a city.
Full of beggars,
A miserable scene breaking the veil of
Holy Lhasa.

拉萨城内又一城，
破篷烁衣连成景。
要问世间何如此？
庙里菩萨不同金*。

A city within city of Lhasa,
Those in rags with broken tents in rows.
Why such a scene?
Buddhas not covered with the same golden color.*

*菩萨的涂料分为纯金粉、人造金粉、铜粉和黄粉

*The different kinds of paint for Buddhas: pure gold, artificial gold, bronze and yellow.

连通拉萨内外的交通要道宇妥桥 20世纪50年代初

Yuthok Zampa connecting the traffic routes inside and outside Lhasa in the early 1950s.

宇妥桥下

饥寒宇妥桥下，
才知到了拉萨城。

Under Yuthok Zampa

Only at the bridge cold and hungry.
Realizing here is Lhasa.

初雪压帐篷，
篷倒一家吼。
哭声盖过风声，
阵阵催人泪涌。

Covered with the first heavy snow,
Tents collapsed with families crying inside.
Cries louder than roaring storm,
Making others' eyes tearful.

衣衫褴褛的老妇 1938年

An old ragged woman in 1938.

天冻，地冻，
空腹愁肠更怕冻。
风冷，雪冷，
冰封乞讨声更冷。
冬寒，春寒，
无家可归人最寒。

The sky frozen, the ground frozen,
Empty stomachs fearful of freezing.
Winds cold, snow cold,
Colder is begging on frozen icy ground.
Winter is cold, and spring is cold,
The homeless feel the coldest.

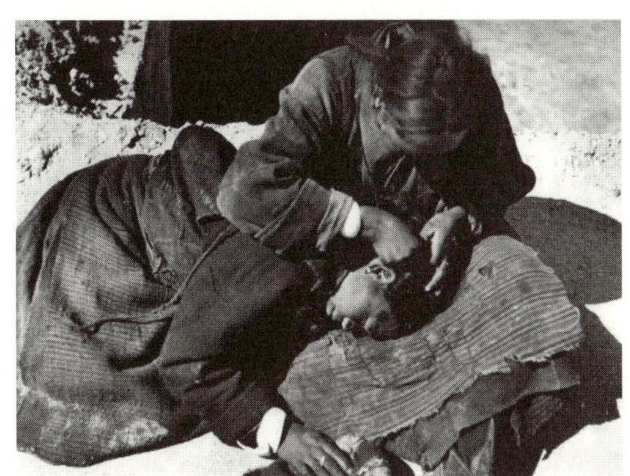

藏族妇女相互捉虱子 1938年

Catching fleas for each other in 1938.

捉虱忙

难逢阳光好，
脱衣捉虱忙。
个个虱子肥带血，
疼在娘心上。

Catching Fleas

Nice sunshine so rare,
Busy catching fleas.
Every flea fat with blood,
Breaking mothers' hearts.

从布达拉宫下的雪村眺望药王山 1938年

Overlooking Chakpori from Shöl Village in 1938.

左边药王山，
右边布宫山，
我们在中间。
药王，神王，
都是高高金顶闪闪，
两山脚下水湾湾，泪也湾湾。
只见帐篷乱，
不见炊烟漫。

拉萨的一个贫困区——鲁固邦仓 20世纪50年代初

A slum named Rugu Bangtsang in Lhasa in the early 1950s.

The Chakpori on the left,
The Potala Mountain on the right,
We are between.
Medicine king, God king,
All glittering on the tops,
At foothills of both, watery puddles with teary eyes.
Only tents visible,
Cooking smoke invisible.

在拉萨行乞多年的双目失明的老人 20世纪50年代中期

The blind old man who has been begging in Lhasa for many years in the mid-1950s.

人间

一个成天伸手讨小钱，
一个衣衫破烂一片片，
一个捂脸哭无泪，
这就是那个年代，
拉萨的风景线。

风景线，
伸延看，
处处凄凄惨惨。
君知否，
是何年？

Man's World

One crying and begging for some change,
One wearing tattered clothes,
One covering the face and crying with no tears,
This was that time,
A scene in Lhasa.

A scene,
With more to see,
More too ghastly to see, more miseries.
Do you know,
What year that was?

捂脸哭泣的老妇 20世纪50年代初

An old woman covering her face and crying in the early 1950s.

在布达拉宫远处扎营的流浪者 1938年

The wanderers who camped in the distance of the Potala Palace in 1938.

圣宫下

冲天处，
是神王住的宫。
入地处，
是你我睡的篷。
天堂地狱命不同，
世间爱钱爱神不容人。

不容人处，
今容人。
帐篷没了，
乞童不见影，
垃圾堆上琼楼明。

Under the Potala Palace

Up in heavens,
Lives God king.
Down on earth,
A tent for you and me.
Different fates in heaven and hell,
Love for money and for gods,
No care for the people.

Where the people once not cared for,
Now with love for them.
Gone are tents,
Gone are beggars,
Fine buildings stand on once trash dumps.

布达拉宫下 2007年 Under the Potala Palace in 2007.

在布达拉宫不远处流浪的儿童 20世纪50年代初 Wandering children not far from the Potala Palace in the early 1950s.

我们的家，	*Our homes,*
紧邻布达拉宫墙。	*Were close to the Potala Palace walls.*
我们的命，	*Our lives,*
就如百孔千疮的烂帐。	*Were like a tent with a hundred holes.*
我们在垃圾堆里生，	*We were born into a garbage heap,*
我们在泥沙窝里长。	*We grew up in dirt and in dirt we slept.*
我们在圣宫下没见爹，	*Outside the holy palace we have never seen our father,*
我们在雄殿下没有娘。	*Outside the holy hall we have never seen our mother.*
风刮帐将折，	*Gales were a terrible melody,*
白雪压倾帐。	*With snow chilled their fragile body.*
拉萨尽荒芜，	*All were bleak and desolated,*
独显达赖王。	*To mirror Dalai Lama the celebrated.*

拉萨进城路上乞讨的一家人 1930年

A family begging on the road to Lhasa in 1930.

天寒地冻，
向你磕头。
云晴风朔，
跪下乞求。
拉萨城里老爷多哟！
酒醉狂欢后，
赐我粥一口。

Cold in the sky and frozen on the ground,
Kowtowing to you.
Dark clouds and blowing winds,
One the knees begging.
In Holy Lhasa so many princes!
Indulgence in drinking,
Spare me a bowl of gruel, please.

卖狗带卖养狗人

市场买狗自来有，
哪有买狗要把养狗人一起买了走？
雪域惊奇多哟，
人都成了商品喽！

买狗的时候要将卖狗人一起买下 1906年左右

Buying dog with its owner as a slave in Lhasa around 1906.

Dogs for Sale with the Owners

Dogs for sale in the market all the times,
But seldom buying dogs with the dogs' owner.
So many strange things in the snow city,
People turned to merchandises.

争食

人与狗争食，
只是说书人嘴里的故事。
哪知拉萨神圣地，
不是故事是事实。
悲剧啊！
人世。

Fighting for Food

For food humans and dogs fighting,
Heard only in story telling.
It happened in Holy Lhasa,
Not stories, but the reality.
How tragic!
On this world.

20世纪50年代初拉萨街头乞讨的残疾人

Disabled people begging in street of Lhasa in the early 1950s.

人与人

社会公平不公平，
去问最下层。
无家可归虽潦倒，
尊严仍可贵。

The Lowest Stratum

Fair or unfair this society,
Go to talk to the lower class.
Though homeless,
Dignified nevertheless.

Lhasa's winter,
Chilly begging chants.
All is misery,
But not so miserable as that
sad face by the street.

Pale clouds high,
Turning around gone was the beggar,
Only people neatly clad.
Time changed,
Poor but with dignity.

藏族妇女 2016年

Tibetan woman in 2016.

酷冻拉萨，
哀声最冷乞声寒。
苦天苦地，
不如那张苦脸。

天高云淡，
如今不见讨钱人，
只有个整洁衣衫。
世道变，
人穷，有尊严。

20世纪50年代初戴着脚镣乞讨的女人
Women begging with shackles on in the early 1950s.

伸手乞讨女，
柳枝青丝长。

似在彩云间，
疑是游天上。

八廓街上的行人 2007年 Pedestrians on the Barkhor Street in 2007.

A hand begging for a woman,
A beautiful figure in a silk skirt.

Like in colorful clouds,
As though touring in the paradise.

风吹破衣臭气扬，
一根打狗棒。
落地咚咚响，
闭眼也猜到。

再睁眼时不一样，
不见打狗棒。
亮亮衫衣处，
真个费思量。

宇妥桥下三位老乞丐和狗 1920年左右
Three old beggars and a dog under Yuthok Zampa around 1920.

Stingy rags in the wind,
A stick in hand to guard against dogs.
Rat-a-tatting on the ground,
Able to guess with closed eyes.

Eyes opened to a different world,
No sticks against dogs,
Nicely dressed,
A sight hard to comprehend.

拉萨的街道 2007年 Lhasa's street in 2007.

布达拉宫前的泥塘 1938年 Muddy pond before the Potala Palace in 1938.

失落的烂泥塘

拉萨泥塘多，
方便打赤脚。
大街热闹处，
好像是过河。
如今都变了，
变成园林城郭。

Missing Muddy Ponds

There were lots of muddy ponds in Lhasa before,
Made people walk barefoot.
Looked like crossing the river
In the busy high streets.
But all these mud gone away,
Becoming enceinte and garden buildings today.

布达拉宫西北的拉鲁湿地 2016年
Lalu Wetlands National Nature Preserve in the northwest of the Potala Palace in 2016.

1904年拉萨的一处水塘 A pond of Lhasa in 1904.

英国人蓝登留下一张拉萨的水塘照，远处的药王山耸立云天。但，几经寻访，就是找不到这个水塘如今在何处。

In the picture of a pond by Perceval Landon, an English man, the Chakpori was visible in the distance. However, the pond is nowhere to be found now. Where did it go?

布达拉宫西北的拉鲁湿地 2007年

Lalu Wetlands National Nature Preserve in the northwest of the Potala Palace in 2007.

八廓街上的普通拉萨民众 1904年

Ordinary Lhasa people on the Barkhor Street in 1904.

“西藏社会死气沉沉，停滞不前。”

——〔美〕梅尔文·戈德斯坦，《西藏现代史（1913–1951）：喇嘛王国的覆灭》

"Tibet society is a lifeless creature, and stagnant."

From ***A History of Modern Tibet (1913-1951), The Demise of Lamaist State*** , by Melvyn C. Goldstein (USA)

八廓街

八廓街，全长一千余米，是一条以大昭寺为中心的弧形街道。有着1300多年历史的八廓街是一条朝圣者用脚步和身体踏成的千年转经路，也是一条见证了许多苦难的道路。

从八廓街上可以望见布达拉宫 1938年
Potala Palace could be seen from the Barkhor Street in 1938.

Barkhor Street

Barkhor Street, with a total length of more than 1,000 meters, is a curved lane centered with the Jokhang Temple. Barkhor Street is a thousand-year-praying lane with a history of 1,300 years that witnessed sweat and suffering of pilgrims.

八廓街两边的商店 2007年 Shops on both sides of the Barkhor Street in 2007.

八廓街 1938年 Barkhor Street in 1938.

街上

泥巴路，百年人生途，
深深浅浅都叫苦。

换了水泥路，
轻快捷足，顺步。
无言，
心有数。
彩衣入画，
云朵如珠。

On the Way

Journey of life, a muddy road,
Full of sufferings deep ahead or shallow behind.

Now paved with cement,
Easy to walk on in smooth steps.
Though no words from the mouth,
All known in the heart.
Pictures full of colorful clothing,
Like pearls are the white clouds.

八廓街 2007年 Barkhor Street in 2007.

八廓街 2007年 Barkhor Street in 2007.

八廓街上摆摊的小贩 1938年 Stalls vendor on the Barkhor Street in 1938.

何由	*Why*
地摊摆在八角坊，	*Spread placed on the Barkhor Street,*
堆笑难招客人来。	*Smile unable to recruit guests.*
断墙哪知饿肠苦，	*Broken walls do not know the pain of hungry people,*
破屋权作避风港。	*With rundown houses as shelters.*

八廓街上热闹的货摊 2007年

Lively stalls on the Barkhor Street in 2007.

拉萨市区街景 1927年
Views from street of Lhasa in 1927.

同一地

牛羊上街，
城乡合一。
酣狗霸地自成趣，
由不得你，
正如那断墙残壁。

Together

Cattle and sheep on the street,
City and countryside united.
The sleeping dog occupying a territory for its own,
Nothing can be done about it,
Just like that broken wall.

拉萨市区的商场 2007年 Shopping malls in Lhasa in 2007.

胡同

多少人走过了，
多少代见证了，
这条胡同。
回头几百年，
屈指数一数，
拉萨的晴与雨，
拉萨的屈与福，
胡同来倾诉。

拉萨姜斯霞路东段（今北京东路） 1957年

East section of Gyantseshar (now East Beijing Road) in 1957.

Alley

So many passed,
So many eye-witnessed,
This alley.
Looking back hundreds of years,
Count them on the fingers,
Lhasa's shine and rain,
Lhasa's fortune and pain,
Let this alley pour out.

拉萨北京东路 2007年 East Beijing Road in 2007.

八廓街上的民居 1937年 Houses on the Barkhor Street in 1937.

惊

半明半暗屋半坍，
火红街市人满。
街同景异不同命，
何因何由何原？

鬼指魍魉弄虚玄，
神示天祖无边。
人说耕耘总在勤，
待君落笔惊断。

Shocked

A house half down and dimly lit,
Crowded street markets.
Same street, different views and varying lives,
Why, why and why?

Ghosts pointing to spirits tricks to play,
God showing the endless sky.
From hard work coming harvest,
Till your writing suddenly stops.

拉萨街边的商店 2007年 Shops on the street of Lhasa in 2007.

八廓街上的碎石堆 1938年
Crushed stones on the Barkhor Street in 1938.

从前落街烂泥滩，
如今艺术村连店。
抬头不见低头见，
请君光临看一看。
雪岭豪情壮志满，
高原新貌暖胜寒。
春花秋月情重，
甸甸颠心田。

Muddy ground in the past,
Arts shops and stores in the present.
Everywhere there are stores,
Inviting you to browse.
Snowy peaks with high aspirations,
Warmth overcoming cold in the plateau.
Spring flowers and autumn moon
Filling the heart with tender feelings.

八廓街 2007年 Barkhor Street in 2007.

西藏民众贩卖纺织品 1929年

Tibetans selling textiles in 1929.

八廓街上经营艺术品的商铺 2007年

Shops selling artworks on the Barkhor Street in 2007.

专营工艺品的商店数量：

拉萨127家，平均200~300个居民有一家工艺品专卖店，这是世界之最。

The number of shops specializing in handicrafts: Lhasa has 127. An average of 200 to 300 inhabitants have a handicraft store, which is the highest in the world.

艺卷长龙一千三★，
花枝好招展，
三里玲珑绿一线。
大千世界渺，
人间奇与冠。

开市去看抢个先，
大昭小昭转★★，
看到日落只一半。
小旗★★★催人走，
留下叹与歉。

八廓街 2007年 Barkhor Street in 2007.

1300 arts and crafts booths,*
So colorful,
1.5 km of colorful exquisites in green lines.
Winding lines of wonders,
Rare and the best in the world.

Be an early bird to the market,
*From the "Big Jok" to the "Little Jok"**,*
Till the sunset covering only a half.
*Little flags *** urge people to move along,*
Only regrets and sighs left behind.

---

*拉萨1300个藏族工艺品的展摊在城区摆成一个长1500米的艺卷。而1951年前，全城没有一个藏族艺术品专营摊。
**大昭，指大昭寺。小昭，指小昭寺。1300个艺品摊位围着大小昭寺等名胜一线排开。
***小旗，旅行团领队的小旗。
*In Lhasa there are 1300 arts and crafts show booths, making an artistic volume of 1.5km in the city. However, before 1951, there was not a single booth specialized in Tibetan arts and crafts in the whole city.
**Big Jok refers to the Jokhang Temple, Little Jok refers to the Ramoche Temple.
1300 booths of arts and crafts are lined along the tourist attractions such as the Jokhang Temple and the Ramoche Temple.
***Little flags refer to tour guides' flags.

拉萨的贸易市场 1921年 Lhasa's trade market in 1921.

八廓街上售卖茶叶的货摊 20世纪40年代
Tea stall on the Barkhor Street in the 1940s.

冷落多年的八廓街北侧“冲赛康”（藏语意为“市场”）重新焕发了活力 1981年
Chomsigkang (means market in Tibetan) on the north side of the Barkor Street, has rejuvenated in 1981 after being deserted for many years.

拉萨的上层人士正招待英国使团成员 1940年

Tibetan dignitaries entertaining some members of the British Mission in Lhasa in 1940.

变化，变化，	*Changes and changes,*
足球，摄影，小汽车，小洋房，小酒吧。	*Football, photography, cars, houses and bars.*
从贵族独占，	*Once only for the nobles,*
到落户大众人家，	*Now for all,*
普度众生顶呱呱！	*Happiness for all!*

八廓街上的餐厅 2014年 Restaurant on the Barkhor Street in 2014.

拉萨繁华地段 2007年 Lhasa downtown area in 2007.

拉萨新建的居民小区 2008年

Newly built residential area in Lhasa in 2008.

第二章

叩近布宫

Chapter 2 At the Potala Palace

旧貌新颜

雪村何在

天梯上下

大门嗟叹

山后兵场暖

山前水野幻

The Old and New Look

Where is Shöl Village

Steps to the Heaven

The Sigh in Sorrow of the Gate

The Warmth Behind the Red Mountain

Lake in front of the Red Mountain

秋日的布达拉宫 2012年 Potala Palace in autumn in 2012.

山前水野幻

Lake in Front of the Red Mountain

布达拉宫东南侧驻藏大臣衙门 1900年左右

Amban's Yamen (Residence of Chinese Official) on southeast side of the Potala Palace around 1900.

叩近布宫从头看，	*At Potala Palace, looking forward,*
风风雨雨几百年。	*Few hundred years of ups and downs.*
谁让天宫破落去？	*Who let the palace go down?*
谁叫新宫动地来？	*Who made the palace anew?*
动地来，	*Anew,*
众人欢，	*All happy,*
心虔诚。	*Be devout.*
一景一物添暖意，	*Feeling warm with nice views and good things,*
雪飘雪融在心间，	*Snow falling and melting in the heart,*
高地不再寒。	*No fear of cold on the highland.*

宫下大泥滩，
要说多烂有多烂。
神王高坐天天看，
永不厌，
悠悠哉哉多少年。
多少年，
烂泥滩配上神圣宫殿。

布达拉宫南侧大片荒地上的泥滩 1900年左右

The mudflats on the vast wasteland on the south side of the Potala Palace around 1900.

Big mires at the palace,
As muddy as they could be.
High above God king looking down,
Not bothered by and tired of,
Idle for so many years,
For so many years,
The sacred palace on muddy puddles.

布达拉宫南侧的泥滩 1938年

The mudflat on the south side of the Potala Palace in 1938.

英军踏过

英军，
千人万脚过泥沼，
雨大一汪洋，
雨小烂泥塘。
今天，
千人万脚寻泥沼，
已不见，
何处访?
风吹绿波起，
云散现绚阳。

英军入侵西藏时踩过的烂泥塘 1904年

Dirty ponds stamped by British troops during the invasion of Tibet in 1904.

The Invasion of British

British troops,
Thousands of feet trod through the swamp,
A vast body of water after heavy rain,
A muddy pond after light rain.
Today,
Thousands of people looking for the swamp,
It is gone,
Where did it go?
In the winds waves the green,
Clouds give way to sunshine.

入侵西藏的英军在布达拉宫下 1904年

British troops under the Potala Palace during the invasion of Tibet in 1904.

当年英军踏过的道路 2007年 The path the British troops used to follow in 2007.

布达拉宫前的大片荒地 1904年
The vast wasteland in front of the Potala Palace in 1904.

Views of water at the Potala Mountain,	布宫山前水野幻，
Once muddy dirt now green land.	泥滩变坦现绿颜。
Why nothing happened for so long but now all changed,	何以亘古今日改，
Singing and dancing in search for reasons.	踏歌吟诗寻由缘。
No need to search,	不用寻，
before are the reasons,	由缘就在你眼前，
Relying on nothing but human beings.	靠人不靠天。

布达拉宫前的广场 2007年 The Potala Palace Square in 2007.

布达拉宫后的藏军军官及士兵在训练 1938年

Tibetan army officer and soldiers training behind the Potala Palace in 1938.

当年神王卫队练兵场，	*Once the drill ground for God king's guards,*
军爷杀声震荡。	*Roaring are soldiers' drill shouts.*
而今林园茂，	*Now enjoyable gardens,*
人闲，天悠。	*People relaxed, heavens relaxing.*
添姿，添妆。	*Color enhanced and beauty added.*

当年的藏军练兵场已经变成绿意盎然的广场 2007年

The training ground has become a greenery square in 2007.

达赖警卫团

按清朝皇帝御准，西藏驻扎军队3000人，其中1000人驻守拉萨，实则为达赖警卫营。辛亥革命清政府覆灭后，西藏政府驱逐了清军，1912年成立了藏军司令部。在英国人的帮助下，西藏军队转为效仿英式，管理、训练、装备均为英式。新式藏军第一团即为达赖警卫团，训练地点在布达拉宫。

Dalai's Guards Regiment

According to the royal emperor of the Qing Dynasty, the Tibetan army should have 3,000 people and 1,000 of whom are stationed in Lhasa. In reality, they are Dalai's security camp. After the Qing government was annihilated in 1911 the Tibetan government expelled the Former Qing Army and set up a Tibetan military headquarters in 1912. With the help of the British, the Tibetan army copied the British way to manage their troops with British administration, training and even equipment. The first Tibetan regiment of the new group is the Dalai guards regiment, the training site was in the Potala Palace.

达赖警卫团的士兵在拉萨姜斯霞路上进行仪仗演习 1940年左右

Soldiers of the Dalai Lama Guards performing ceremonies on Gyantseshar around 1940.

信徒们围绕布达拉宫叩头祈愿 1956年

Believers praying around the Potala Palace in 1956.

同一斜阳桥，
不同情映照。

前一张，
两重宫墙外，
人众赶程忙。
抢在落日前，
进城占个避风巷* 。

布达拉宫广场步行道 2007年

Footpath in Potala Palace Square in 2007.

后一张，
遮阳抬头望，
信步数风光。
恰畔花径水，
白塔妖娆绿中藏。

---

*旧西藏时期多数人到拉萨城后，没有钱住店，常找巷里墙下避风处栖身过夜。

*Many Tibetans could not afford hotel rooms after arriving in Lhasa. They often slept at lane walls to keep from the wind.

布达拉宫广场步行道 2007年 Footpath in Potala Palace Square in 2007.

The same small bridge at dusk,
In two different pictures.

In one,
Outside the two palace walls,
People hurrying on their way.
Before the sunset,
To take shelter of walls from the wind.

In the other,
Covering the sunlight to look up,
Walking relaxedly and enjoying the view.
Flowers along the water banks,
Deep in the green hiding the white pagodas.

夜晚的布达拉宫广场喷水池 2010年 Palace Square fountain in the night in 2010.

布达拉宫入口处 1938年

Entrance to the Potala Palace in 1938.

布宫入口一幅画，
多少苦力被践踏。
烂泥垃圾一地，
断墙破屋水洼。
访客搭车过，
叩头人在哪？

A picture of the entrance to Potala Palace,
How many slaves passed by.
Littered with dirt and trash,
Broken walls, run-down homes and muddy puddles.
Visitors' bus passing,
Where to find kowtowing people?

“差巴”将晒干的山羊和牛送入布达拉宫 1938年

Serfs sending dried goats and cows into the Potala Palace in 1938.

布达拉宫入口处的水洼 1904年
Puddles of water at the entrance to the Potala Palace in 1904.

布达拉宫入口处 1958年 Entrance to the Potala Palace in 1958.

鲜花簇拥的布达拉宫 2010年 Flowers blooming around Potala Palace in 2010.

污泥林园化，	*Mires gardenized,*
绿意全拉萨。	*All Lhasa gardenized.*
坦坦阳光道，	*Smooth streets,*
红花竞黄花。	*Red flowers competing with yellow,*
辛苦汗滴处，	*All from hardworking sweat,*
悠悠尽绿华。	*All into green.*

布达拉宫广场 2007年 Palace Square in 2007.

布达拉宫旁的宗角禄康公园 2016年

Dzongyap Lukhang Park beside Potala Palace in 2016.

天梯上下

布达拉宫天梯 1938年 Steps to the Potala Palace in 1938.

踏着天梯上天宫，	*On the heavenly steps to the heavenly palace,*
心潮难平复。	*With mixed feelings.*
既有神王又有奴，	*Be both God king and slave,*
人间天上穷。	*Miserable down on the earth and up in the heaven.*

旧西藏“差巴”往布宫运货物

Serfs sending goods to the Potala Palace in the past.

Steps to the Heaven

神王上天你我抬，
你我梯破入地来。
千年石板皆有灵，
一片高原白。

天梯上的僧侣和支差的藏民 1938年

Monks and serfs on the steps to Potala Palace in 1938.

布宫天梯 2016年 Steps to the Potala Palace in 2016.

You and I carried the God king to the heaven,
You and I broke the steps to go to the hell.
The flagstones carved with our souls,
All is pure in the highlands.

雪村何在

Where is Shöl Village

布达拉宫下的雪村 20世纪50年代初

Shöl Village under the Potala Palace in the early 1950s.

从布达拉宫俯瞰雪村 1938年

Overlooking Shöl Village from the Potala Palace in 1938.

雪村 1938年 Shöl Village in 1938.

通过红山前的烂泥水域向布达拉宫走去，最先进入视线的是巍巍宫墙外一片矮小、参差不齐的藏式民居，这就是“雪村”（原称“山下村”，又称“下村”）。

“雪村”因外观与布达拉宫“太不合拍”被拆除，改为绿茵草坪。

然而，一些人撰写专文，指责拆除“雪村”是“大汉主义”鄙视藏式民居建筑艺术。

由于“雪村”已拆，死无对证。“雪村”所代表的“西藏文化艺术惨遭绝灭”，好像是铁定了。

但是，“雪村”又重新出现在以下的画面中。

有道是：

“雪村”紧连圣宫墙，
百姓企盼沾神光。
沾了吗？
几张旧照见周张？

雪村中的监狱，囚犯戴着木枷 1920年

Shöl Dekyiling, where prisoners were detained with wood shackles in 1920.

Passing the muddy puddles at the foothills of Marpori (Red Mountain), outside of the magnificent walls of the Potala Palace, one would first see small irregular-sized Tibetan-style houses, known as "Shöl Village". (Formerly known as "Foothill Village", also called "Low Village")

The "Shöl Village" was torn down due to their being unharmonious with Potala Palace, and was transferred into green lawn.

However, some people wrote articles to criticize the tearing down of the "Shöl Village" as being "Hanist" and as despising the artistic style of Tibetan architecture.

Because the "Shöl Village" is now gone, there is no evidence to check against, "The art of Tibetan culture represented by the 'Shöl Village' has been destroyed", as though it were a fact.

Nevertheless, the "Shöl Village" appeared in this picture.

As it goes:

The "Shöl Village" linked to the palace walls,
People wishing some luck from God kings.
Any luck? Only the old pictures would tell.

信徒匍匐在即将被拆除的雪村外 1966年

Believers crawling around Shöl Village which was about to be removed in 1966.

“雪村”房子四尺高，
爬进屋内依墙靠。
难熬今夜风暴，
总胜街头流浪。

Four feet high are the houses in the Snow Village,
Crawling into the house and leaning against the wall.
Hard to pass tonight's storm,
Still better than roaming about on the street.

“雪村”新颜 2016年 New look of Shöl Village in 2016.

旧貌新颜

The Old and New Look

布达拉宫和红山 20世纪初

Potala Palace and Marpori in the 1900s.

几张布宫旧照，
一张不如一张，
有道是：
朝日红火落日黄。

These old pictures of Potala Palace,
Getting worse.
As it goes,
Bright red sunrise leading to faded yellow sunset.

1924年的布达拉宫 Potala Palace in 1924.

布达拉宫墙垣上的乌鸦 1938年

Crows of the Potala Palace in 1938.

布达拉宫白宫 1980年

Potrang Karpo ("White Palace") in 1980.

布达拉宫红宫维修现场 1989年

Repair site of Potrang Marpo ("Red Palace") in 1989.

布达拉宫维修现场的工匠正在修复雕刻 20世纪90年代

Craftsmen repairing carving of the Potala Palace in the 1990s.

布达拉宫始建于公元7世纪吐蕃王朝藏王松赞干布时期，距今已有1300年的历史。

吐蕃王朝灭亡之后，古老的宫殿大部分毁于战火，加上雷击等自然灾害，布达拉宫的规模日益缩小，

1645年，布达拉宫重建，并在之后的300多年里，不断得到扩建。

1961年，布达拉宫被列入第一批全国重点文物保护单位，每年都会进行维修与保养，俗称“岁修”。

截至目前，规模较大的维修有两次。第一次是1989年至1996年的历时7年的大维修，称为第一期工程（国家累计拨款5500万元）。在中国文物与古建筑保护的历史上，这是史无前例的工程。1994年12月17日，布达拉宫正式被联合国列入《世界遗产名录》。第二次是2002年至2010年的以加固地垄为主的巩固性工程，称为第二期工程（国家拨款1.79亿元）。

Potala Palace was first built in the 7th century during the reign of Tubo king Song-zan Gan-po, and has a history of 1300 years.

After the fall of the Tubo Kingdom, most of the old palaces were destroyed by war, and with the natural disasters such as lightning strikes, the scale of the Potala Palace was shrinking.

In 1645 the Potala Palace was rebuilt. Over the next 300 years, it has continued to expand.

In 1961, the Potala Palace was included in the first batch of Cultural Relics of National Priority Protection units, and maintenance was carried out every year, commonly known as “Yearly Repairs”.

Up to now, there have been two large-scale maintenance projects, the first of which was from 1989 to 1996. The seven-year-long maintenance was called the first phase of the project. (The state has allocated a total of 55 million *yuan*.) This is an unprecedented project in the history of the preservation of Chinese cultural relics and ancient buildings. On December 17, 1994, the Potala Palace was formally listed by the United Nations on the "World Heritage List". The second is the consolidation project mainly consisting of reinforced ridges from 2002 to 2010. It is called the second phase of the project (the state allocated 179 million *yuan*).

拉萨民众参加布达拉宫广场扩建工程 1995年

Lhasa people participating in the expansion of the Potala Palace Square in 1995.

工程技术人员在加固维修布达拉宫新发现的地垄 2008年

Engineers and technicians reinforcing and repairing newly discovered ridges in the Potala Palace in 2008.

几世惆怅已过去，
瞬间新宫起。
我们来躬身叩地，
宠儿也欢喜。

天梯神宫喜新装，
待我远客造访。
昔日恶臭已成忆，
风抚绿茵飘香。

布达拉宫前叩头祈愿的信徒 1938年

Believers praying before the Potala Palace in 1938.

Melancholy of generations is gone,
New Palaces are erected.
Let's bow and kowtow,
The pet dog is content.

Steps to heaven and palace of God decorated grandly,
Awaiting my visit.
The stench past is history now,*
Green woods stroked by wilds with sweet fragrance.

布达拉宫前叩头祈愿的信徒 1997年

Believers praying before the Potala Palace in 1997.

远眺布达拉宫 1903年

Overlooking Potala Palace in 1903.

布达拉宫西北偏西 1900年左右

Potala Palace from West-Northwest around 1900.

红嘴鸥

圣宫脚下滩水漫，
酣酣几千年。
可怜人常吃不饱，
谁管大自然？

荒原丛野改作园，
花海畔堤岸。
人爱山水终有报，
红鸥送春远。

宗角禄康公园湖中的红嘴鸥 2016年 Red mouth gulls in the lake of Dzongyap Lukhang Park in 2016.

Red Mouth Gulls

Puddles at the foot of the sacred palace,
For thousands of years.
Starving were the miserables,
Who cared for Nature?

Wilderness turned into gardens,
Flowers along the lake banks.
Those loving mountains and rivers will be rewarded,
Red-mouthed gulls bringing back spring.

雪山环抱中的布达拉宫 1938年

Potala Palace surrounded by snow mountains in 1938.

雪原大换颜，
拉萨出新天。
白日金顶闪，
夜来总月满。
那不是月圆，
是布宫的光环。
曲水笑容焕，
荒山变青山，
这不是苏南是曲南。

New face of snowland shines.
New look of Lhasa arrives.
The golden roof glistens in the day light,
A full moon always hangs up during the night.
Oh, it is not the full moon,
But halo of Potala Palace.
Kyichu River is elated and bright,
Barren hill becomes green and alight.
This is not China's Jiangnan, the most beautiful place,
But the city of sunlight.

雪原虔诚重，
中原华情浓。
两原同一缘，
同献中国梦。

The piety of the snow-plain is earnest,
The affection of the central plain is profound.
The relation of the two plains is predestined,
To have the same one Chinese dream refound.

夜幕中的布达拉宫 2016年 Potala Palace in the night in 2016.

布达拉宫 2015年 Potala Palace in 2015.

布宫前有一片茵茵绿草
绿
是希望
布宫上有一片碧碧蓝天
蓝
是关怀
绿蓝映西藏
天天成长

布宫前有一片绿
野风起浪
好像我的床
引我入梦乡
布宫上有一片蓝
苍云飘荡
好像是云裳
迎我进天堂

In front of Potala Palace is green grass,
Greenness,
Is hope.
Above Potala Palace is blue sky,
Blueness,
Is care.
Greenness and blueness decorate Tibet,
And much more will come.

In front of Potala Palace is greenness,
The wind gently pushes the river waves,
As if a swing-bed
Cradling me into a dreamland.
Above the Potala Palace is blueness,
Floating clouds arises.
As if a dress,
Greeting me to the paradise.

布达拉宫白宫 2016年 Potrang Karpo ("White Palace") in 2016.

地绿天蓝好风光，
布达拉宫世向往。
何以景颜今胜夕，
鬼斧神工新思想。

The green land and blue sky form a good background,
All people love Potala Palace and wish to come around.
Its charming scenery is the best of all times,
New thoughts and new ideas are profound.

第三章 北望大昭

Chapter 3 Looking Northward at Jokhang Temple

金顶之间

大昭大

唐蕃会盟碑

大昭关与开

The Golden Rooftops

The Magnificent Temple

Monument of United Tang and Tibet

The Opening and Closing of Jokhang Temple

拉萨大昭寺 20世纪80年代 Jokhang Temple in the 1980s.

大昭关与开

The Opening and Closing of Jokhang Temple

大昭寺门口 1940年左右

Entrance to the Jokhang Temple around 1940.

昭，光明。大昭，大光明。但，不尽然。

1940年间，在英国人拍摄的照片中，就有好几张录下了年节时的情景：大昭寺的大门用木板封闭，人们不得从其门而入。

Jokhang, the Temple of the Lord, in Chinese it means brightness. While it is not always the case.

The following photos taken by a British photographer around 1940 shows that the gate of the Jokhang Temple was blocked by wooden planks.

大昭寺门口木板紧闭 1938年

Closed door with wooden boards in 1938.

英国人兰登拍摄的大昭寺正门 1904

The main entrance to the Jokhang Temple by Perceval Landon in1904.

英国人兰登拍摄的大昭寺 1904

Jokhang Temple by Perceval Landon in 1904.

大昭寺广场 2007年 Jokhang Temple Square in 2007.

大昭寺大门完全重开的年代，在西藏地方政府的档案中查不到记录。

十四世达赖喇嘛两次清空布达拉宫地库逃往印度，而绝大部分大寺院住持和各地官贵也卷财而去。丢下的烂摊子，令大昭寺几乎财气尽失。

直到20世纪80年代，得益于改革开放后的长期“全国援藏”，大昭寺出现了空前的人潮、磕头潮。

No evidence can be found in Tibet's official history before 1950's record to show any period of time when the gate of Jokhang Temple has been reopened.

The 14th Dalai Lama cleared the fortunes from the Potala Palace and escaped to India twice. The abbots of monasteries and local officials also robbed the palace and ran off. The Jokhang Temple almost lost its wealth.

It was not until the 1980s, thanks to the long-term “National Aid to Tibet” after the Reform and Opening-up, now the Jokhang Temple has become a popular place for pilgrims and tourists.

1984年的大昭寺广场 Jokhang Temple Square in 1984.

大昭寺门口 20世纪40年代

Entrance to the Jokhang Temple in the 1940s.

自由，
自由，
有钱寺门自由开，
没钱大门钉下板，
自由莫进来。
年节跳神好去处，
此时看神不要钱。

Freedom,
Freedom.
With money the monastery gate was freely opened,
Without money the gate was nailed with planks,
And freedom was shut outside the gate hardened.
Festival was a good place for holy dances,
And to see the holy spirits at this time was free of expenses.

英军入侵西藏时的大昭寺前 1904年

Entrance to the Jokhang Temple during the British invasion of Tibet in 1904.

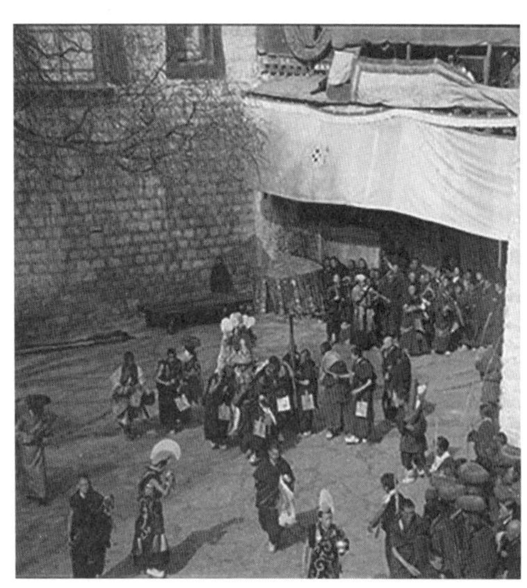

大昭寺门口 1940年左右

Entrance to the Jokhang Temple around 1940.

帷也烂，
地也陷，
危墙险。
挂起床单送客，
三五朝圣人散。
人心散，
虔心酸，
回家转。
神前孤灯何冷！
信众举步何艰！

The curtain was worn,
The ground was worn,
The wall was collapsing.
The curtain hung, guests gone,
The few pilgrims were leaving.
Thought unfocused,
Heart distressed,
Pious people were homeward going.
In front of the statue many bright lights were not found,
At the gate congregations were not abounded.

虔诚的朝觐者 1938年

Pious pilgrim in 1938.

大昭寺前的僧侣和孩童 1938年

Monks and children in front of the Jokhang Temple in 1938.

丢掉生皮袍子，
穿上现代纺织。
身换衣衫人换颜，
精神文明进行时。

Drop rawhide robes,
Put on modern textiles.
From changed clothes to changed faces,
Spiritual civilization is progressing.

大昭寺广场上的行人 2016年

Pedestrians on the Jokhang Temple Square in 2016.

大昭寺前的朝拜者 2016年 Pilgrims in front of the Jokhang Temple in 2016.

大昭门前，	*In front of the Jokhang Temple,*
全是拜垫。	*Full of mats.*
镜左镜右，	*From left to right,*
人影攒。	*Full of people.*
长跪长磕东方事，	*Since it's freedom to kneel and kowtow in the East,*
何以西方有人怨?	*Why is there complaint in the West?*

大昭寺广场前的朝拜者 2010年 Pilgrims on the Jokhang Temple Square in 2010.

不是年来不是节，	*Neither a festival nor event,*
无约无束四方来。	*Coming from far and near unfettered,*
万众聚散秩而序，	*Millions of people gather and dismiss in order.*
虔诚忠诚动地哀。	*The devoutness touched heaven and earth.*

唐蕃会盟碑

Monument of United Tang and Tibet

唐蕃会盟碑的碑文 1957年

Inscription on the Monument of United Tang and Tibet in 1957.

大昭寺前的唐蕃会盟碑 1921年

Monument of United Tang and Tibet before the Jokhang Temple in 1921.

汉藏会盟立天誓，
不偏不倚如此石。
千年霹雳有多少，
风也是诗雨也诗。

The Han and Tibet established this monument as an oath to heaven,
Pledging to be just and firm as this stone with oath woven.
The millennium has witnessed numerous thunder storms,
It knows the gales and rains are part of epic too.

雪域拉萨朝拜行，
汉传藏传本大乘*。
一千万人俱归来，
汉情藏情撼天庭。

Going on a pilgrimage trip to Lhasa,
The Hans and Tibetans follow Mahayana.*
Ten million pilgrims come to worship the Buddha,
They express their love of each other in front of the altar.

唐蕃会盟碑前的信众 2013年
Believers in front of the Monument of United Tang and Tibet in 2013.

共高原，
昆仑上下山绵雪绵。
共云天，
中华苍穹月缺月圆。
生命出一线，
汉也藏，
藏也汉。

They share the great plateau,
And its stretches of snowy mountain.
They share the sky with white clouds,
And half moons and full moons on the firmament of the Nation.
Tibetan and Han,
Han and Tibetan,
Are from one life fountain.

共姻联，
代代相约手牵梦牵。
共患难，
风雨同舟荣辱同担。
东西共天下，
春秋几千年。

Intermarriage repeated,
They go hand in hand for generation and generation.
Weal and woe shared,
Through storms they are in the same boat with consolidation.
Living together for thousands of seasons,
They have made no alternation.

*汉传佛教与藏传佛教，均属大乘佛教。

*The Han Chinese Buddhism and Tibetan Buddhism are both Mahayana Buddhism.

大昭大

大昭寺前准备煨桑的朝拜者 1938年

Pilgrims preparing for blessing ceremony in front of the Jokhang Temple in 1938.

月昭华，
日昭光，
大昭更明朗。
你添颜，
我添笑，
染得满城亮堂。

Sunlight,
Moonglory,
Jokhang Plaza more bright.
All smiles,
All laughs,
Making the whole city brilliant.

The Magnificent Temple

Gray building dotted with red spots,	万般梵烟几点红，
People hidden in the crowds,	人在群中隐，
Heads moving in the insect smoke.	头在群中踊。
"Four elements", what are they?	四大皆空所何指，
Happy people meeting in bright colors.	五光十色喜相逢。
Who says one feels chill in a high position,	谁说高处不胜寒，
Tibetan snow is the whitest,	藏雪最白，
Tibetan girls are the prettiest.	藏姑最艳。

拉萨的煨桑仪式 1987年

Blessing ceremony in Lhasa in 1987.

The same pilgrimages,	朝拜依旧，
Only changes in clothes.	只是服饰改。
Smoke of Buddhism thickened,	梵烟犹盛，
Only missing is the golden sedan chair.*	独缺黄轿抬*。
Bluer is the Lhasa's sky,	拉萨更蓝了，
How beautiful!	美哉！

*黄轿抬，指十四世达赖喇嘛所坐的24人抬的金顶大轿，大昭寺是神王和噶厦政府的办事地。

* With the top of the chair painted gold, the golden sedan chair was used by the 14th Dalai Lama, which was carried by 24 men. Jokhang Temple is the site of the God King and Kashag government.

金顶之间

The Golden Rooftops

大昭寺的金顶 1938年 Golden rooftops of the Jokhang Temple in 1938.

大昭金顶朔风寒，	*Cold wind over the golden rooftops of the Jokhang Temple,*
日晒雪蚀逾千年。	*With sun exposure and snow eroding for over a thousand years.*
人间倾榨无时了，	*There is endless exploitation in the world,*
又谁重修添金还？	*Who has money to rebuild and add gold to the sacred temples?*
时换月换年也换，	*Time changes everything,*
高原终于出新天。	*The Tibetan plateau finally emerged a new day.*
金顶大修重光耀，	*Golden rooftops shine again after repairs,*
喜了千家万人脸。	*The Tibetan people all have happy faces.*

大昭寺的金饰 1938年

Gold ornaments of the Jokhang Temple in 1938.

近年来，尤其是2013年至2014年，西藏黄金金粉销量出现井喷。金粉大多数用于寺院的大门、寺顶、主柱和佛像等重要部位的修建或者大修。黄金金粉销量的井喷，真实地反映了西藏寺院信众以及寺院收入的大量增加。

In recent years, especially from 2013 to 2014, sales of gold paint in Tibet caught up with a spurt of fast growth. This is because most of the gold paint is used for overhaul of important parts such as gates, temple tops, main columns and Buddhist statues of monasteries. This blowout of gold paint consumption reflects the substantial increase in the number of believers and their dedication to the monastery.

经过鎏金工艺维修的大昭寺金顶，在柔和阳光的照耀下熠熠生辉 2014年

Golden rooftops of the Jokhang Temple shining under the sunlight after sheet metal repair in 2014.

自五世达赖扩建以来，经过300年的日晒雨淋，大昭寺的金顶已黯然失色。2011年启动了有史以来最大的大昭寺金顶维修工程，总面积达3743平方米，金顶鎏金所使用的金子难以估价。

Since the expansion of the fifth Dalai Lama, after 300 years of sun and rain, the golden rooftops of the Jokhang Temple have been overshadowed. In 2011, the largest maintenance project of golden rooftops of Jokhang Temple in the history was launched, which covered an area of 3,743m^2. The gold used in the golden rooftops is difficult to value.

大昭寺 2014年

Jokhang Temple in 2014.

第四章

喇嘛王国

Chapter 4 Kingdom of Lamas

新潮涌

铁杆兵

千僧面

南辞林卡

神王

New Trend

Gekor Monk

Faces of Monks

Leaving the Norbulingka

The God King

大法会上的普通僧侣 20世纪50年代中期

Ordinary monks on Monlam Prayer Festival in the mid-1950s.

身着丝绸长袍的僧侣 1938年 Monks dressed in silk robes in 1938.

普通僧侣的生活条件极其恶劣，其穷困之状，非文字可以形容。
——英军侵藏指挥官荣赫鹏

"The ordinary monastic life was particularly bad; their life is despaired which no words can adequately describe."
From Captain Younghusband (The commander of British invading troops to Lhasa, 1904)

十三世达赖喇嘛在罗布林卡接见国民政府文官刘曼卿 1930年

The 13th Dalai Lama meeting with the National Government officer Liu Manqing in Norbulingka in 1930.

蹉跎岁月不知晓，
55年风雨任缥缈。
所留身影何相异，
多身京装*“八字胡”**，
寄予人想。

Letting time slip by without knowing it,
55 years of raging storms.
Photos left behind were not that different,
Mostly dressed in Beijing-styled clothes and
wearing "八-shaped" mustaches.

十三世达赖喇嘛

The 13th Dalai Lama.

十三世达赖喇嘛与查尔斯·贝尔（左）1910年

The 13th Dalai Lama and Charles Bell (left) in 1910.

晚年的十三世达赖喇嘛 1933年

The 13th Dalai Lama in his late years in 1933.

*京装，指当时北京的官服，即长袍马褂。

**“八字胡”，民国时如孙中山、袁世凯、黎元洪等人都留八字胡。

*Beijing-styled clothes refer to the clothes worn by officials at that time: gowns and vests.

**"八-shaped" mustaches were worn by some of the national leaders such as Sun Yat-Sen, Yuan Shi-Kai and Li Yuan-Hong.

十三世达赖喇嘛乘坐的八抬大轿 1921年
Eight-lift sedan of the 13th Dalai Lama in 1921.

两个神王*不同轿，
后来者居上：
又是锦衣卫，
又是圣伞，
又是华兴，
又是抬官**凤凰帽。
好一个威风了得的新神王！
只可惜，
山荒，
地黄。

*In different sedans are two God Kings, **
The later, look imposing:
Guards in brocade,
With sacred umbrellas,
In grandeur,
*With phoenix crown of the sedan carrying officers**.*
What a majestic new God King!
The only shame,
Hills barren,
Fields desolate in yellow.

十四世达赖喇嘛出行 1958年
The 14th Dalai Lama travelling by sedan in 1958.

---

*指十三世达赖喇嘛和十四世达赖喇嘛。
**抬官：达赖喇嘛大轿的抬轿人。
*The 13th Dalai Lama and 14th Dalai Lama.
** Carrying officers: the sedan carriers for the Dalai Lamas.

锦衣铁蹄响，
呼拥过神王。
室外叩礼乱，
屋内饿断肠。

吹燃一炉红火，
洒染一山幽绿。
再借东风*在手，
平和逛市场。

十四世达赖喇嘛的金轿巡行 1940年

The golden sedan of 14th Dalai Lama travelling in 1940.

Rumbling passing cavalry soldiers in brocade,
Thundering chanting passing the God King.
All outside on the knees disorderly kowtowing,
All inside were starving.

Red fire in stove,
Bringing green to the mountains.
*With "Eastern Wind", **
Shopping leisurely in markets.

骑摩托出行的藏族妇女 2007年

Tibetan woman travelling by motorcycle in 2007.

---

*指“东风牌”摩托车。

*Referring to motorcycles of "Eastern Wind" brand.

罗布林卡的格桑颇章 1957年
Kelsang Podrang of Norbulingka in 1957.

十四世达赖喇嘛住的罗布林卡，位于拉萨河畔的水网地区。

Norbulingka, where the 14th Dalai Lama lived, was located in the water network area of the Kyichu River.

罗布林卡内达赖喇嘛的宝座 1938年 Dalai Lama's throne in Norbulingka in 1938.

罗布林卡环水亭 约20世纪初

The Dragon King Pavilion in Norbulingka around the early 1900s.

龙王守湖竟无水，
百朱河歌依旧，
天命随水流。

Protected by Dragon King,
A waterless lake.
Songs of the river sounding the same,
Flowing with the destiny.

罗布林卡环水亭 约20世纪40年代

The Dragon King Pavilion in Norbulingka around the 1940s.

罗布林卡 2014年 Norbulingka in 2014.

措吉颇章*没我无水，
大昭无我不亮。
西藏少我天将塌，
再待那将军**求驾。

圣湖水回涨，
大昭更明亮。
喜山昆仑擎天柱，
断肠人魂飘那乡。

措吉颇章 1957年 Tsokyil Podrang in 1957.

Without me, no water in the Tsokyil Podrang,*
Without me, Jokhang Temple not shining,
Without me, the sky in Tibet falling,
*Waiting for the General ** to ask me again.*

The Holy lake water rising,
Jokhang Temple shining,
The Himalayas and Kunlun,
Upright pillars supported the sky,
Where is the soul of the one with a broken heart?

措吉颇章 1999年 Tsokyil Podrang in 1999.

---

*措吉颇章，罗布林卡内的湖心亭。1959年3月17日十四世达赖喇嘛出走时，罗布林卡的内湖无水。
**将军，指1950年十四世达赖喇嘛第一次出走后，中央人民政府派张经武将军专程赴亚东劝达赖返藏。

* Tsokyil Podrang, the mid-lake pavilion of Norbulingka. When the 14th Dalai Lama fled on 17th March, 1959, the inner lake of Norbulingka dried out.

** The General means General Zhang Jingwu, he went to Yadong In 1950 to persuade the 14th Dalai Lama to return to Lhasa after Dalai's first fleeing.

金色颇章 1938年 Chensil Podrang in 1938.

钟停摆

人去楼未空，
只是访客换了神态，
换了容。
碧天蓝透，
菊黄花更红。

金色颇章 2005年 Chensil Podrang in 2005.

十四世达赖喇嘛离开罗布林卡逃亡印度的时间是1959年3月17日晚上9时，现在这个老钟仍指向这一时刻。

The 14th Dalai Lama left Norbulingka to India at 9:00 p.m. on March 17th, 1959. Up to now, the clock still stays at 9:00.

Clock Stopped

The people gone,
But the room not empty,
Only visitors' expressions changed,
So blue is the sky,
Yellow chrysanthemum turning redder.*

千僧面

大昭寺前的僧众 1938年

Monks in front of the Jokhang Temple in 1938.

信仰自由不自由，
不在别人口，
只在人心头。

Religion, free or not free,
Not because the others call it,
But because it is in the people's heart.

心里自由不自由，
不在嘴巴溜，
只在脸上留。

Deep in the heart, feeling free or not free,
Not in words,
But on the faces.

Faces of Monks

Feeling	**感**
Pictures of monks	众僧相，
Are different.	前后有两样。
50 years ago	50年前：
Feeling cold,	寒战，
Cuddled up.	缩一团。
A half rice ball and a half bowl of gruel,	饭团半个粥半碗，
Looking at me and looking at you,	大眼望小眼，
Cold, helpless and speechless.	冷无奈处也无言。
50 years later	50年后：
Beaming with joy,	眉开，
Laughing together,	笑成团，
When hopeful,	心有所系梦也甜。
Dreams are sweet.	

僧众正在进行法事活动 20世纪90年代

The monks holding rites in the 1990s.

辩经 1938年 Monastic debates in 1938.

辩经

看辩经人的脸，
判辩经人的心。
看四下人的笑多少，
知四下人的情。

喇嘛们正在辩经 20世纪80年代 Monks debating in the 1980s.

Monastic Debate

From the speaker's face,
Know his heart.
From the laughs and smiles around,
Know their feelings.

Corners of the mouth

Your long face and my smiling face,
Which is more attractive?
Your pouted mouth and my rounded mouth,
Which is sweeter?

Dare to ask why?
Time advanced;
Mind changed.

嘴角

你的板脸比我的笑脸，
哪个中看？
你的嘴扁对我的嘴圆，
哪个心甜？

敢问为什么？
时代先后，
换岁改年。

阳光下苦苦祈祷的僧侣 1938年
A monk praying hard in the sun in 1938.

法会上的老僧 20世纪40年代 Old monks at a prayer meeting in the 1940s.

情

为何这多苦脸？
为何这多笑颜？
不在天高地厚，
心畅一笑自然。

Emotion

Why so many sad faces?
Why so many smiling faces?
Not because the sky is high and earth is deep,
But because smiling gets to their hearts' content.

法会上的僧侣 2016年 Monks at a prayer meeting in 2016.

僧侣以经商维持生计 1956年

Monks earning their living by doing business in 1956.

生计

锁紧眉头看，
苦心佛陀盼。
不知也不觉，
悍马*太阳能家私一展。
一展问青天，
神王已走远，
又来何方神仙。

色拉寺僧侣用太阳能灶烧水 2006年

Monks in Sera Monastery using solar cooker to boil water in 2006.

The Living

Looking with knitted brows,
Awaiting the Buddha.
Not aware,
*A show of "Hummer",**
Solar energy and furniture.
Asking the blue sky,
Gone is the God King,
Here comes an immortal from nowhere.

---

* “悍马”，名牌汽车。
* "Hummer", a famous car brand.

铁杆兵

大昭寺中的铁棒喇嘛，众僧莫不俯首听命 1957年

A Gekor monk in the Jokhang Temple holding a long stick, and other monks all bowing down in 1957.

一根大棍有多长？
总在你我头上见。

How long is the stick?
Hovering over our heads.

Gekor Monk

铁棒喇嘛所经之处，众僧皆退避三舍 1938年

When Gekor monks arrived, other monks all going out of the way in 1938.

铁棒喇嘛 2015年 Gekor monks in 2015.

铁棒喇嘛，藏传佛教中僧人之称谓，亦称“格贵”“纠察僧官”“掌堂师”。主要掌管各个寺院或扎仓僧众的名册和纪律，也是负责维持僧团清规戒律的寺院执事。常随身携带铁杖，故得名。相当于汉传佛教寺院的护法武僧。

Gekor, the title of monks in Tibetan Buddhism, also known as Executive Officer, Peace Officer, or Branch Officer. They are mainly in charge of each Monasteries or Zhacang monks' roster and discipline, but also responsible for maintaining the rules and prohibitions of the monastic monks. They often carry an iron stick, which is why they got the name. Gekor is equivalent to the Peace Officer monk in Han Buddhism monastery.

大法会上使用iPad和iPhone的僧侣 2016年
Monks using iPhone and iPad at a prayer meeting in 2016.

用iPhone的僧侣 2016年 A monk using his iPhone to record in 2016.

拉萨街头使用笔记本电脑的僧侣 2006年

Monks using laptop on the street of Lhasa in 2007.

就怕你看错，
“寸头*”，计算机，
满街过。
拉萨城虽老，
鲜活事儿多。
见怪不怪，
新时代太快，
风云也蹉跎。

In case you are mistaken,
"Inch-haired", computers,*
all over streets.
Old as Lhasa may be,
Not lacking are new things.
Not alarmed by strange sights,
New times rapidly advancing,
Winds and clouds chasing.

---

*按佛寺规定，出家人不能留发，必须将自己头上的戒疤示人。

*Every monk should show his discipline points on head according to the temple's regulations.

拉萨近郊的云游僧人 1936年
A walking monk in the suburbs of Lhasa in 1936.

搭乘卡车的僧侣 2001年
A monk taking a truck in 2001.

云僧

云游僧，没寺的和尚，
破袈裟，漂泊走天涯。
折枝，
相依以为命，
伴随在脚下。
茫茫云海，
巍巍唐古拉。
踏破铁鞋，难有
我的寺，
我的家。

突然机器声，
驾车代步伐。
云僧说“再见”，
迎面烟弥沙。

Walking Monks

Walking monks, no temple's monks,
In worn-out cassock, roaming around.
A branch as a stick,
Accompanying the feet,
Sea of clouds and the towering Tanggula Mountain.
Travelling till shoes worn out, still no
My temple,
My home.

Suddenly, machines running,
Driving replacing walking.
"Good-bye", say walking manks
To the smog and dusty sand.

愫尼

死板的脸变羞羞，
羞羞的脸上加笑容。
笑容的脸擦口红，
脱下红衣聚亲朋。

Buddhist Nun

Stiff faces turned into shy ones,
Shy faces with smiles,
Lipstick on the smiling faces,
Off deep red cassock, partying with friends and relatives.

拉萨尼姑讲解佛的故事 1920年
A nun explaining the story of Buddha in Lhasa in 1920.

藏族妇女 2007年 Tibetan women in 2007.

第五章 朝圣之路

Chapter 5 On Pilgrimages

漫漫通天路

昼朝夜拜

殿堂内外

悲悯世界

Long Journey to Heaven

Worship Day and Night

Inside and Outside of the Temple Hall

The Miserable and Sympathy

转经的藏族老妇 2016年 An old Tibetan woman praying in 2016.

哀莫大于心死，
爱莫大于无我。

No grief greater than hopelessness,
No love greater than selflessness.

背着孩子赴拉萨朝圣的藏族妇女 20世纪30年代

A Tibetan woman carrying her child to pilgrimage to Lhasa in the 1930s.

刻在脸上的岁月，
历历在寸间。
不用开口问，
已知出何年。

Years carved on the faces,
All in between inches.
Need not open the mouth to ask,
Already know the age.

藏族老妇人 2016年 An old Tibetan woman in 2016.

拉萨街道上的居民 1904年
Residents on the street of Lhasa in 1904.

八廓街上的流浪者 1938年
Wanderers on the Barkhor Street in 1938.

样貌

一面面愁容对笑容，
一副副沉重对轻松。
这是为什么？
我爷问天，
我妈问地，
我们问自己。

Faces

Worried faces against smiling faces,
Heavy burdens against pleasures,
Why is that?
Grandpa asks the heaven,
Grandma asks the earth,
We ask ourselves.

英军侵藏沿途所见藏民 1904年

Tibetan people along the way during the British invasion of Tibet in 1904.

神志

从脸孔，
看人心。
东风或是西风，
霜降或是雪落。
愁喜苦乐？
统统刻在脸上，
入木三分有多。

欣赏文艺节目的民众 20世纪90年代

Tibetan people enjoying art programs in the 1990s.

Frame of Mind

From the face, see the heart.
Eastern winds or western winds,
Frost or snow.
Happy, worry, bitter or sweet?
On the face all carved,
More than three-inch deep into.

心地

日月转，
命也转。
婴儿的笑，
娃子的脸。
千万莫回头去想，
莫回头去看。
想了心酸，
看了寒战。

日喀则集会上的男女老幼 1938年

Men, women and children at a country fair of Shigatse in 1938.

Mind

The sun rotating and the moon rotating,
So is life.
Baby's smile,
On a child's face.
Don't turn back to think,
Don't turn back to look.
It'll make you sad to think,
It'll make you shiver to look.

法会场上的男女老幼 2016年 Men, women and children at a prayer meeting in 2016.

情所在

笑得多好，笑得多爽，
笑得蓝天归我。
笑得眉开，
心飞云霄上，
翔！

老农奴和她的孙儿 1937年

An old serf and her grandson in 1937.

哥哥背弟弟 1998年

A Tibetan boy carrying his little brother on his back in 1998.

Hope On

What a good smile,
What a hearty smile.
The smile bringing me the blue sky.
Melting my face in smiles,
Flying my heart up into the skies,
Fly!

想知人们心上事，
看脸不看脚。
要问快乐不快乐，
一扫众嘴角。
不妨试一试，
保你猜个准着。

拉萨近郊的贫穷牧民 1938年
Poor herdsmen in the suburbs of Lhasa in 1938.

Things to the heart,
Showing on face not on feet.
Happy or not,
Showing on corners of mouth.
Try it you may,
You will guess right for sure.

那曲的牧民 20世纪60年代 Herdsmen of Nagqu in the 1960s.

转动经筒的老人 1938年

An old man turning his prayer wheel in 1938.

转动经筒的老人 2012年

A group of old people turning their prayer wheels in 2012.

会名堂而皇之何多，	*There are all kinds of meetings,*
“经筒大会”几曾见过？	*But have you seen the meeting of prayer wheels?*
婷婷经轮对人众，	*Turning wheels facing each other,*
谁唱主角谁配角？	*Who plays the main character?*
忆当年，	*In the past,*
千人一个*只因破，	*One prayer wheel in a thousand people just because of poverty,*
破衣破产人破落。	*Clothes ragged and people undecent.*
看如今	*Today,*
人手一个只因阔，	*One prayer wheel per one person just because of being rich,*
阔天阔地身腰阔。	*Wallet bulging and people decent.*

---

* 20世纪50年代西藏人口100多万，共有小经筒不及千只；如今西藏330多万人口，平均六七人一只经筒。

* In the 1950s, Tibet had a population of over 1 million with prayer wheels less than a thousand. Today Tibet has a population of over 3.3 million, with every six or seven people having a prayer wheel on average.

Wrinkles on this face,
Deeper than those on the next one.
This person's stories,
Sadder than the next one's.
Hoping this year better than the last one,
Wrinkles fade on younger generations.

前一个面孔皱纹，
比后一个深陷。
前一个人的故事，
比后一个心酸。
一年比一年好些吧，
后来人的皱褶渐淡。

转山 20世纪40年代 Circumambulation in the1940s.

转山 20世纪90年代 Circumambulation in the1990s.

Two groups of people circumambulating the mountains,
Two different kinds of faces,
Why sad faces changed into smiling ones?
Ah!
Time has changed,
Time marches on!

两群转山人，
张张脸，
何以苦脸转成了笑脸？
啊！
风翻云也翻，
时光不流连！

左看，右看，
一只风符塔，零零风马带。
你脸，我脸，
仿佛是一张张
几曾相似的画面。
串来，挤去，
时隐时现。
看你，看我，
喜笑挂上脸，
欢乐尽染。

拉萨大法会 1929年
Monlam Prayer Festival in 1929.

Looking left, looking right,
A paper ribbon of scripts, several prayer flags.
Your face, my face,
Like those familiar paintings.
Squeezing in and out,
Appearing and disappearing from time to time.
Looking at you, looking at me,
Smiles on the faces,
Joyful together.

冬天的法会场 2016年 A prayer meeting in winter in 2016.

三个奶奶

三个老奶奶好虔诚，
第一个
锁眉细问命运，
第二个
数指盘算今生，
第三个
安宁静入神韵。

法会上的老奶奶 2015年
A Tibetan old granny at the prayer meeting in 2015.

Three Grandmothers

How reverent the three grannies are,
The first
With knitted brows, asking about her destiny,
The second
On the fingers, thinking about her life.
The third
In peace, enthralled by her tranquility.

藏族老奶奶 2016年
A Tibetan old granny in 2016.

藏族老奶奶 2016年 A Tibetan old granny in 2016.

布达拉宫外的朝圣者 1938年

Pilgrims outside the Potala Palace in 1938.

寒风，泥地，宫窗，
愁容，散发，苦肠，
祈祷人在断墙。

Chill winds, muddy roads, palace windows,
Anxious look, messy hair, broken heart,
A prayer at a broken wall.

站在寺庙顶楼的喇嘛 1938年

A Lama standing on the top floor of a temple in 1938.

守卫在寺庙门前的武僧与藏獒 1938年

Armed monks and Tibetan mastiffs guarding the temple gate in 1938.

英军军官（中间站立者）1904年

A British officer (standing in the middle) in 1904.

鞭

英国人不高，
偏要站在大大的石头上。
西藏人不矮，
却躬身于长长的皮鞭下。

大石头搬走了，
英国人和他的长鞭也影消。
大昭寺前人人平等，
大堂更明亮。

Whip

The English were not tall,
But still standing on high rock.
Tibetans were not short,
But still bowing to the long whip.

Removed are the big stones,
With their whips and the Brits are gone.
Before Jokhang Temple equal for all,
Brighter is the great hall.

外国游客在藏族导游带领下游览大昭寺广场 2007年8月9日

Foreign tourists visiting the Jokhang Temple with Tibetan guides on Aug. 9, 2007.

鞋破了，袜子也破了，
有人的衣服烂。
跪伏在地上，
像是牲畜席地卷，
不见老天来可怜。
此景此律几百年，
何时完？

何时完？
在今天：
换了新鞋，
有了垫子，
衣服好体面。

Shoes worn out, and so are socks,
Someone's in rags.
Kneeling on the ground,
Like an animal rolling on the ground,
No pity from gods.
This scene of hundreds of years,
When would it end?

When would it end?
It ends today:
In new shoes,
On new mats,
In decent clothes.

大昭寺前带着孩子磕长头的信徒 20世纪50年代

A believer kowtowing in front of the Jokhang Temple with her child in the 1950s.

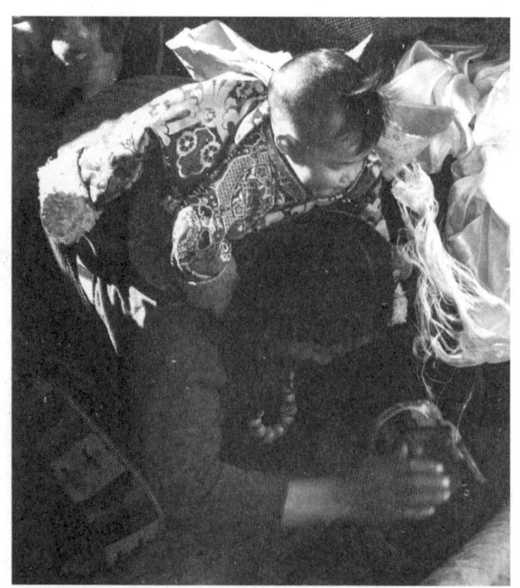

背着孩子磕长头的信徒 2015年

A believer kowtowing with her child on her back in 2015.

纺羊毛线的母女 1938年

A mother and her daughter spinning woollen thread in 1938.

经轮

祖母锁眉经筒转，
母亲愁容挂上脸。
我把毛线卷，
祈神，赚钱。

Cylinder

Grandma spinning the prayer wheel with knitted brows,
Mother's worried look on her face.
But yarn threads I am reeling,
For pray, also for money.

转经筒的老奶奶 2014年

A Tibetan old granny turning her prayer wheel in 2014.

大昭寺前磕长头的信徒 20世纪60年代

Believers kowtowing in front of the Jokhang Temple in the 1960s.

祈求

60年代祈求，

80年代等候，

90年代应验了：

手表，戒指，皮绒……

小孙孙悠悠。

大昭寺前磕长头的信徒 2007年

Believers kowtowing in front of the Jokhang Temple in 2007.

Praying

Praying in the 60's,

Waiting in the 80's,

Fulfilled in the 90's.

Watches, rings, leather and fur coats…

Grandson is happy.

磕长头 2007年 Kowtowing in 2007.

我的命	*My life*
比前人幸运，	*Better than older generations,*
我的心	*My heart*
比前人虔诚。	*More pious than older generations.*
生活一天天好起来了，	*Life better and better each day,*
我就是见证。	*The witness I am.*

昼朝夜拜

黎明前的大昭寺 2016年 The Jokhang Temple before dawn in 2016.

拉萨的黎明，	*The daybreak of Lhasa*
离天最近。	*Is the closest to Heaven.*
黎明的大昭，	*The auroral lights of Jokhang*
就在我心。	*My heart enlighten.*

夜幕中绕大昭寺转经的信徒 2016年

Believers praying around the Jokhang Temple in the night in 2016.

Worship Day and Night

夜拜，拉萨一景，世界一画。全世界朝圣都在白天，独有拉萨于2014年涌现大批夜拜人，开启朝圣奇观。拉萨从晨曦初现，就拉开了一天的朝圣序幕。

The nighttime pilgrimage is the unique scenery of Lhasa, and it is even particular all over the world. Pilgrimages are usually done in the daytime, only Lhasa has witnessed many people who come to worship in the nighttime since 2014. From first rays of the morning sun, a day's pilgrimage starts.

天色未亮，大昭寺前已是信徒云集 2016年

Believers gathering in front of the Jokhang Temple predawn in 2016.

高原雪港云上船，	*Sailing on cloud and snow-covered plateau,*
艘艘小舟大昭前。	*These little boats finally port in front of Jokhang.*
左边是藏右是汉，	*The Tibetans are on the left and the Han right,*
横空渡世大华天。	*They share the vast land of China.*

携家带口前往大昭寺的信徒 2016年 Believers going to the Jokhang Temple with their families in 2016.

莫道君行早，
虔诚试比高。
车步赶在前，
争献头炷香。

Busy walking in the early morning,
They compare piety for significance.
Striding forward eagerly,
They wish to offer the earliest incense.

大昭寺前的朝拜者 2016年 Believers in front of the Jokhang Temple in 2016.

举起双手迎朝阳，	*Hands raised to welcome the morning sun,*
东方最明亮。	*The east shines the brightest.*
一片虔诚祈天地，	*Piety prays to Heaven,*
寄语最情长。	*And heartfelt words are sincerely sung.*

世界第一条环城磕头专线
The First Route around the City of Kowtowing in the World

八廓街上磕长头的信徒 1957年

A pilgrim kowtowing on the Barkhor Street in 1957.

夜幕降临，朝拜人还在专线上磕长头 2016年

As night fell, the believer still kowtowing on the dedicated route in 2016.

拉萨是世界上第一个为磕头信众开设专线的城市，八廓街道中辟出一条浅色的叩头专线 2016年

Lhasa is the first city in the world to open a dedicated route to kowtow for believers. A light-colored path was set up on the Barkhor Street in 2016.

围城环绕转经道，
一拜一叩一佛修。
那时候
无雨风沙走，
雨雪泥淋稠。
饥寒肠将断，
鲜见绕城修。

On the beltway around the road of the Scripture Wheel,
Pilgrims bowed, kowtowed step by step to worship.
At that time,
Wind blew up sands in the days of no rain,
And the road became muddy in the days of snow.
Stomachs ached because of coldness and hunger,
Kowtowing was seldom seen around the city.

但如今
青石路面笑雪风，
叩头专线举世优。
环城转经白天满，
“夜拜奇观”呈新犹。

But today,
The green stone road surface laughs at the wind and snow,
A world's best road has been built for kowtowing.
Wheel spinners fill the city during the day,
And a new spectacular scene of evening worship warms the night.

朝圣者身旁的柳树被认为具有神圣力量 1938年

Next to the pilgrims was the willow tree which was believed to have sacred power in 1938.

虔诚的朝拜者 1938年

A pious pilgrim in 1938.

想了又想：
在从前，
王就是神，
神就是天，
统掌阴阳两权。
如今是，
人人是王，
洗沐换面，
阳光雨露温暖。

Think and think again:
Before,
A king was the god,
Controlling my earthly life and spiritual life.
Today,
I am king and so is each of us.
Bathed in warm sunshine and rain of the Grace,
Feel my radiant spirit in peace.

转山 2016年

Circumambulating mountains in 2016.

这张无奈的年轻脸，
这身补疤的破皮衫。
这片荒地，
从我门外就枯干，
何年有灵泉？
这条登天路，
从我祖上就走起，
何时才走完？

有灵泉，
就在你的心间。
有终点，
就靠你的虔诚。

拉萨进城道路上虔诚的朝圣者 1938年

A pious pilgrim on road to Lhasa city in 1938.

This hopeless young face,
This broken leather coat with patches.
This desolate yellow land,
So dry right from my door step,
Where is the water spring?
This road to the heaven,
Travelled by my ancestors,
Where is the end?

The water of soul,
Right in your heart.
The end,
Only on your piety.

虔诚的朝圣者行进在公路之上 2016年

Pious pilgrims crawling on the road in 2016.

我在前跪倒，
你在后跪倒。
风尘万里一生了，
藏亲汉戚寺前早。
月圆月缺，
路程知多少，
历史烟云何绸缪。

面向神山圣湖跪拜的朝拜者 1938年

Pilgrims kowtowing before the sacred mountain and holy lake in 1938.

I kneel down in front,
You kneel down behind.
A journey of thousands of miles in dusts lonely,
Bring Tibetans and Hans to the monastery as in one family.
Full moon and waning moon repeated.
Miles and miles were covered,
The smoke of history mutably rose and lingered.

转山 2016年 Circumambulating mountains in 2016.

拉萨杨树大道旁虔诚的朝拜者 1938年

Pious pilgrims on Lhasa Poplar in1938.

八廓街上店铺如云，朝圣者、行人川流不息 2016年

Barkhor Street had many shops and endless flow of pedestrians and pilgrims in 2016.

人拥人，只为
朝圣拉萨城。
磕长头的伏成串，
前面的脚，快要
顶住后面人的脸。

也来朝圣又逛街，
更多的是来
上学求知，
探亲会友，
交易赚钱，
晴空万里无边。

People pushing around,
Only for pilgrimage to Lhasa.
Lines of kowtowing pilgrims,
Feet of the people ahead, nearly
Touching the faces behind.

On a pilgrimage and for shopping,
More for schooling and learning,
Visiting relatives and friends,
Trading and money-making,
Under boundless blue sky.

第六章

天路

Chapter 6 Heavenly Road

忘乎南山
记乎渡口
苦旅

Forgetting Nanshan
Remembering Ferry Dock
The Suffering Journey

经青藏铁路，从北京开来拉萨的火车 2007年 A train from Beijing to Lhasa along the Qinghai-Tibet Railway in 2007.

苦旅

曲水上的铁索桥 1904年

Iron bridge over Chu-shur in 1904.

狰狞藏道难，	*Tortuous are roads in Tibet,*
悬在断崖边，	*Cut in halfway up the mountainside.*
木桩支不稳，	*Supported with tree branches,*
摇摇晃晃荡秋千。	*Back and forth like a swing.*
秋千命难长，	*Swinging with short lives,*
摇晃险不堪。	*Swaying with bitter lives.*
后退藤条断，	*Rattans will break if you go back,*
如果想活不想死，	*If you want to live,*
只能冒险走上前！	*Just move forward.*

The Suffering Journey

翻山越岭的商队 1938年

A caravan over the mountains in 1938.

公元641年，唐文成公主嫁给吐蕃王，从长安出发，用了两年才到达。

清朝共派出123位“驻藏大臣”，在这些高官中，有9人死于赴任途中。

1930年，民国政府官员刘曼卿去拉萨与十三世达赖喇嘛会面，从成都出发，骑马45天到达。

In 641, the Tubo king married princess Wencheng of the Tang Dynasty who arrived in Tibet after a two-year journey from Chang'an.

The Qing Dynasty sent a total of 123 "Officials to Tibet", of whom nine died on their journey to Lhasa.

In 1930, Liu Manqing, a National Government officer, was sent to Tibet to meet the 13th Dalai Lama. It took Liu 45 days on horseback to get to Lhasa from Chengdu.

国道318上的72道拐 2015年 72 turns onto the mountain on National Highway 318 in 2015.

农奴主外出时骑在农奴背上 20世纪40年代

Serf owners rode on the back of the serfs when they went out in the 1940s.

骑人

老爷“支差”要骑我，
害怕泥巴脏了脚。
世道真沧桑，
有脚不走路，
骑人才快活。

Ride on Me

On my back the master setting out,
In fear of dirt getting on his feet.
How strange!
With feet, but walking not,
Happy on my back.

我背老爷不言累，
老爷骑我要息腿。
茶点摆正先奉上，
老爷怕风我挡吹。

No complaining about carrying the master on my back,
Having a rest for a while after being on my back.
Setting up tea and snacks for the master,
I block the wind for the master.

Carried a God

Walking whips in hands,

Officials in silk clothes guarding on sides.

God King sitting in the sedan carried by 24 men.

Reverent!

Dignified!

Birds droppings on the golden tower,

Common people standing in the cold winds.

Nothing but whipping sounds can be heard,

Here comes the whip,

Skin open!

Motorcycles aside,

Happily meeting one another

All people are equal in the snow country,

Hugging,

All together!

抬神

执鞭开路走在前，

锦官护两边。

二十四人抬轿神王坐，

多神圣，

威严！

金塔鸟粪堆满，

百姓风里寒。

万肃只听长鞭响，

看鞭到，

肉绽！

摩托机车靠边，

重逢喜相见。

雪域雪白人平等，

紧拥抱，

成团！

十四世达赖喇嘛乘轿出行 20世纪50年代中期

The 14th Dalai Lama travelling by sedan in the mid-1950s.

跳起节庆的舞蹈 2005年 A festival dance in 2005.

山

脊背弯，
背了一座山。
主人家还嫌少，
双眼横目一横鞭。

不用弯腰不用赶，
没人横目不见鞭。
只听雪地吱吱声，
原来是
驴踩初雪踏破冰。

不堪重负的农奴 20世纪中期

Serfs overwhelmed by a heavy burden in the mid-20th century.

Mountains

On the bent back,
Carrying a mountain.
Still not enough for the master,
An angry glare with a whip in hand.

No need to bend the back, and not to be driven,
No angry glare and no whips.
Only the sound from snowy ground,
By
The donkey on the snowy and icy roads.

牵着毛驴背木柴的藏族小孩 20世纪90年代

A Tibetan child holding a donkey with firewood on back in the 1990s.

换了汽车在手，
风驰电掣。
披星戴月昆仑山，
明天拉萨再见。

The steering wheel in hand,
Running flashing fast.
Over the Kunlun Mountain in the moonlight,
See you in Lhasa tomorrow.

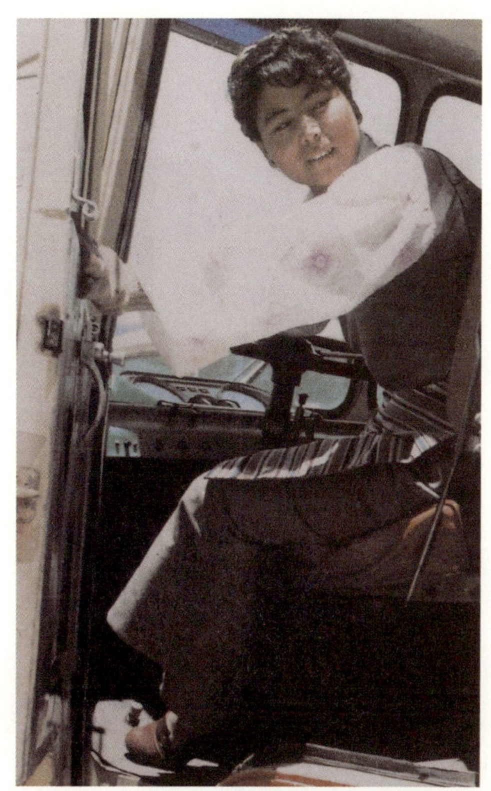

20世纪80年代的拉萨公共汽车女司机
A female bus driver of Lhasa in the 1980s.

记乎渡口

拉萨河渡口的皮筏 1938年
Skin rafts on Kyichu River ferry in 1938.

一只划子渡河去，
抛下一片水漫烟愁。
幽情堤岸伴流水，
别有一番风景在画中！

One boat crossing the Kyichu River,
All was left behind.
Sentimental banks by flowing water,
A unique view in the picture!

拉萨河大桥 2014年 Kyichu River Bridge in 2014.

Remembering Ferry Dock

拉萨河 1959年 Kyichu River in 1959.

拉萨河 2007年 Kyichu River in 2007.

拉萨南山 1959年 Nanshan in 1959.

过南山，
南山已去远。
南山依旧在，
反又
山添了绿，天添蓝。

Over the Nanshan,
Far away the Nanshan appears.
Still standing there is the mountain,
Only now
The hill is greener and the sky bluer.

拉萨南山公园 2016年 Lhasa Nanshan Park in 2016.

杨树大道 1938年 Poplar Avenue in 1938.

杨树大道 2007年 Poplar Avenue in 2007.

通往拉萨的大道 1938年 Road to Lhasa in 1938.

拉萨市区四通八达的道路 2014年 Roads of Lhasa leading in all directions in 2014.

自行车 *Bicycles*

十三世达赖喇嘛的宠侍扎西顿珠（骑车人）和两名贵族子弟 20世纪30年代

Tashi Dondru, servant of 13th Dalai Lama (cyclist) and two noble children in the 1930s.

骑着自行车去做朝拜的拉萨市民 2007年

Residents of Lhasa riding bicycles to make pilgrimage in 2007.

小轿车 *Cars*

1957年在亚东，农奴将贵族从印度购买的汽车拆成零件翻越乃堆拉山口抬回拉萨

1957 in Yadong, the serfs dismantling the car bought by the nobles from India into parts and climbing over the Nathra Pass to return to Lhasa.

拉萨的私人汽车数量，1920年至1952年为3辆，1970年为17辆，2010年约80,000辆。

The number of private cars in Lhasa was 3 from 1920 to 1952, 17 in 1970 and about 80,000 in 2010.

拉萨街头的小汽车 **2011**年 Private cars on the street of Lhasa in 2011.

第七章

恰是景颜改

Chapter 7 As the Colors of Views Changed

藏北双湖嘎措乡的牧民新房 2002年

New houses of herdsmen in Gamtso County, Shuanghu, Northern Tibet in 2002.

20世纪70年代的拉萨太阳岛
Sun Island in the 1970s.

太阳岛是拉萨河上的一个大岛，有河相隔离。原来的太阳岛满目荒凉，是乞丐、流浪者聚集的地方。后来经过统一的规划，太阳岛现在成了由餐馆、酒吧、茶室、宾馆、手工业加工、政府部门组成的花园。

The Sun Island is a large island isolated by the Kyichu River. Many beggars and wanderers in Lhasa used to go to this desolate place in the past. Now under the Government's plan it transformed to a garden composed of restaurants, bars, tea rooms, hotels, handicraft processing, and government departments.

2007年的拉萨太阳岛 Sun Island in 2007.

太阳岛，

黄旦旦，

太阳光下火烧滩。

夏日水泛，

冬冻寒，

冰封连到山。

水坝起，

洪水拦，

栽树株株心与汗。

夏日浇灌，

冬燃烟，

茂密新江南。

拉萨太阳岛 2016年 Sun Island in 2016.

The Sun Island,

Yellowish,

Scorching hot under the sun.

Water overflowed in the summer,

Bitterly cold in the winter,

All frozen to the mountains.

Dams built,

Floods blocked,

Trees planted with care and sweat.

Watered in the summer,

Making fire in the winter,

Like Southern China covered with luxuriant green.

拉萨以西的拉萨河 1900年左右

Kyichu River, west of Lhasa around 1900.

西藏是世界上水资源最丰富的地方，有落差最大的河流。拉萨，就坐落在拉萨河畔。但是，20世纪50年代以前，拉萨人用水还是靠人力背送。

Tibet has the richest water resources in the world including rivers with the greatest drop in the world. Lhasa is located at the side of Kyichu River. However, all domestic drinking water had to be carried by human to Lhasa before the 1950s.

拉萨居民从水沟里取饮用水 20世纪50年代初

Residents of Lhasa taking drinking water from a ditch in the early 1950s.

Carrying water,

Heart broken with every step.

Water carried for food,

Child left behind crying piercing my heart.

A drop of milk is grain of wheat!

My child,

Mom's tears are much more than the long water flow.

支差背水的藏族妇女 1950年以前

Tibetan woman who had to carry water for living before 1950.

背水娘，
一步一心伤。
背水去换粮，
丢下娃儿嚎断肠。
一滴汗水一粒谷啊！
我的儿，
娘的泪水更比河水长。

拉萨背水的藏妇 20世纪40年代

Tibetan women carrying water in Lhasa in the 1940s.

地上的石头，
磨穿了我的脚趾头。
飕飕的北风，
刮得我黄脸枯瘦。
娃子的哭叫，
震得我步步颤抖。
背水女的奴隶身，
由不得自己。
管家人的皮鞭长，
你走到哪里，
跟到哪里。

背水妇将水倒入寺庙前的大铜鼎内 20世纪50年代初

A Tibetan woman pouring water into a large copper tripod in front of the temple in the early 1950s.

拉萨村民在院子里取用干净的自来水 1994年

A villager in Lhasa using clean tap water in the yard in 1994.

大昭寺内院的自来水龙头 2007年
Water tap in the Jokhang Temple in 2007.

The rock on the ground,
Grinding on my foot toes.
Whizzing northern winds,
Blowing my face pale and bony.
Cries of children,
My steps were shivering with the cries.
As a water-carrying slave,
Having no freedom.
The master's long whips,
Follow you,
Wherever you go.

大昭寺内院的排水井盖 2007年
Drainage well covered in the Jokhang Temple in 2007.

牧野春田

原野上的农奴和牦牛 1900年左右

Serfs and yaks on the field around 1900.

Spring Fields

汉藏人民在市郊挖坑种植柳树和杨树 1955年

Han and Tibetan people digging pits in suburbs to plant willows and poplars in 1955.

搬开石头堆成行，
赢得大片好河床。
全藏动手植千树，
育出高原新苏杭。

Rocks piled in rows,
Making nice river beds.
All Tibet mobilized to plant trees,
Creating Suzhou and Hangzhou on the plateau.

植树造林 20世纪70年代 Afforestation in the 1970s.

山南错那地区使用木棍和铁锄翻耕土地 20世纪50年代初

Wooden sticks and iron hoes used in ploughing in Cona of Shannan in the early 1950s.

改天换地，
木棍木犁换了机器。
老皇历黄了十多个世纪，
也该退休了吧，
找个角落歇息。

Transforming heaven and earth,
Wooden sticks and plows replaced by machines.
Old almanac is over ten centuries,
Time to retire,
Getting a place to rest.

洛隆县的藏民用现代化机械收割粮食 21世纪

Tibetans in Luolong County harvesting grain with modern machinery in the 2000s.

Chains

In the field handcuffed,
In rags shaking in the wind.
Helpless on the shaking field,
Holding on to the hoe sighing.
Who to save me?
The god?
The heaven?

Gone are iron chains and rags,
Green trees and highland barley and
yellow flowers.
All changed and human became wiser.
New technologies all over the highlands.
Grateful to whom?
Destiny of emancipation.

铁链

戴上铁链下田，
几丝烂衫风里颤。
地动山摇无助，
扶住锄把喘又叹。
谁救我呢?
神吗?
天?

铁链丢远，
树绿稞青黄花璨。
地改天，
新技术添彩高原。
谢谢谁呢?
命运
身翻!

农奴主怕农奴逃跑，强迫农奴戴着锁链劳动 1950年以前

Before 1950 serf owners usually chained their serfs to keep them from running away.

西藏堆龙德庆区羊达村农业技术员晋美（右）在指导村里的藏族群众防治小麦病虫害　2003年

Agricultural technician Jigme (right) from Yangda Village, Doilungdêqên County, Tibet, guiding villagers to control wheat diseases and pests in 2003.

妇女们按质量筛选青稞 20世纪50年代初

Women sorting Tibetan barley by quality in the early 1950s.

选

排排坐，选青稞。
好的送到老爷的仓，
差的放进牛簸箩，
最坏的才是我的口粮。

满园青稞，属你属我。
青春脸上映红霞，
笑个够，对天歌。

Engaged in Labour

Sitting in rows, selecting Tibetan barley.
The good sent to the master's barn,
The bad to the owner's cowsheds,
The worst is my food.

Now all the barley in the yard is yours and mine.
Youthful faces reflecting beautiful sunshine,
Laughing to the heart's content, and singing to the sky.

拉萨市达孜区迎来丰收 2007年8月

Dagzê County had a good harvest in August, 2007.

群羊

举起羔羊祈向天，
雪海不如羊群长。
不堪回首不会忘：
恢恢旷野，
风起骸骨响。
想来泪汪汪，
哭断肠……

Flocks

Holding up a lamb to pray,
The sea of snow smaller than my flocks.
No looking back and can't forget:
So cold the wilderness,
Bones'sound with striking winds.
Tearful when recalling,
Crying till heart broken...

捧起羊羔的牧童 1982年

Shepherdess holding a lamb in 1982.

Dyeing

A big yellow mountain,
Without trees a barren mountain.
With hard work and efforts of all,
Smiling rainbow in the dusk light.

山川染

一座大山美，
无树一山光。
难挡众人志，
虹霞笑夕阳。

察隅地区雨后的彩虹 1956年

A rainbow after the rain in the Zayü area in 1956.

药王山西北坡 1900年左右 Chakpori from northwest around 1900.

药王山 *Chakpori*

山崖岭下土坡黄，
千年不毛以为常。
以为常事今不再，
一山青绿已苍苍。

Below the cliffs and ridges is yellow soil,
Not abnormal when no plants growing.
Once usual no more now,
A view of green is all you may see.

药王山下 2016年 Under the Chakpori in 2016.

藏北赛马会上的流动货摊 2007年

Mobile car stall in a horse event in northern Tibet in 2007.

沙洲

包袱挂在车尾巴，
走风沙。
身上是沙，一脸沙，
沙原黄坡沙送沙。

汽车商店到我家，
车篷货箱洁无沙。
大人小孩拥上前，
彩色衣衫如虹霞。
沙地出绿芽，
大美藏野如画。

Sand

Bags hanging at the back,
Travelling westward.
Sand on body, sand on face,
All desert sand over sand.

Mobile shop coming to my home,
Car roof and goods boxes free of sand.
Old and young all pushing forward,
Colorful clothes like beautiful rainbows.
Seedling out of sand,
Picturesque Tibet resembling a painting.

农奴的晚餐。农忙时，农奴们从黎明便开始劳动，直至深夜才得到一餐粗粝的豌豆糌粑 20世纪50年代初

In the early 1950s, dinner of serfs. During busy farming season, the serfs at manor continued to work from dawn until late at night before they were given a rough meal of pea pods.

盘中餐

仿佛来到集中营，
仿佛又见难民群。
空空大碗，
哪有饭团，
用力手抓也枉然。

天转地转命也转，
大盘大盘菜和饭。
同庙同殿，
相去何远，
就是菩萨也惊叹。

寺庙中丰盛的自助餐 2005年

Fine buffet in the temple in 2005.

Eating

As if being in a concentration camp,
As if seeing refugees again.
Empty big bowls,
No food in them,
Grasping hard in vain.

The heaven changed, the earth changed and life changed too,
Plenty of food in big plates.
The same temple and the same hall,
Why so different,
Even Buddha is exclaiming!

席地成团，
改为餐桌餐院。
望眼欲穿，
换了盆盆菜选。
饮食文化，
不用手抓夹起筷子拣。

Setting on the ground then,
Setting at tables now.
Not enough to eat then,
Enjoying gourmet food now.
The dietary habit has been much better,
No more eating with hands,
Using chopsticks now.

五级电工卓嘎邀请汉族师傅到家做客吃饭 1980年

Level 5 electrician Cholga inviting her Han mentor to eat at home in 1980.

僧侣用筷子夹盆盆菜 2007年 Monks using chopsticks to select food in 2007.

住在山洞里的农奴 20世纪50年代初

Serfs living in a cave in the early 1950s.

一排“房子”几个洞，	*A row of homes in caves,*
一个洞儿一家人。	*A cave is a family.*
风吹刮起土，沙满屋，	*When the wind blowing dust fill homes,*
雪来堆住洞，冰凌凌，	*When snow falling, doors blocked, icy cold inside,*
苦啊！命！	*It's abyss of misery!*

堆穷*阿男一家挤在又小又暗的破屋中 20世纪50年代初

Anan, a düjung serf, crowding into a small, dark house with his family in the early 1950s.

*堆穷，1959年前的农奴等级之一。

*Düjung, a grade of serfdom before 1959.

栖身厕所下，
是人不如牛和马。
官贵高入云，
还有神王大喇嘛。

住在厕所下面的“朗生”*次仁卓玛 20世纪50年代初

“Nangtsen” Tserin Cholma living under the toilet in the early 1950s.

次仁卓玛住在庄园主的马棚里 20世纪50年代初

Tserin Cholma living in the stable with the master's horses in the early 1950s.

Sheltered under the roof of a toilet,
A person, but less worthy than a livestock.
The wealthy and nobles living in high clouds,
And so did the God King and great lamas.

---

*朗生，即奴隶

*Nangtsen means slave.

山南庄园拉加里 1957年

Lagari Manor in Shannan in 1957.

庄园

这大的花园楼是谁家？
这小的狗儿洞住哪娃？
高楼对上洞，
西藏一张画。

Ranches

Owner of this grand villa who was?
Living in this small doghole who was?
Tall building and holes,
A picture of Tibet.

一个猫臭洞，
便是我的家，
进出弯身爬。
飞雪夜难眠，
抱狗取点暖。
苦待东方明，
可怜我这娃。

A smelly cat cave,
Which is my home,
Made me bend to crawl in and out.
Snow and winds accompanying long nights,
Holding the dog for keeping a little bit warm,
Waiting the sun coming up,
Showing mercy to me the poor kid.

娃子住的洞穴 20世纪50年代

"Wazi"- serfs living in these caves in the 1950s.

庄园的娃子

你是哪家的“娃子”*?
哪个是你的主人?
你在哪家的债簿上?
哪家庄园的苦丁?

农奴的居所，冬不蔽风夏不避雨 20世纪50年代初

A serf's house could not shelter wind in winter nor rain in summer in the early 1950s.

Ranch's wazis

Whose "wazi" are you?*
Who is your owner?
In whose debt book are you?
Which manor are you enslaved by?

---

*1950年前，藏人初相识时，第一句话不是问名字，不是说住址，而是问“你是哪家的娃子？”即是问：“你是哪家的奴隶？”

*Before the 1950's, when Tibetans met for the first time, the first words they said were not to ask the names, nor addresses, but to ask "Whose wazi are you?" It means "Which manor are you enslaved by?".

次仁拉姆 *Tserin Lhamo*

山南结巴乡农民次仁拉姆将11户最穷的朗生组织成互助组，在田间劳动，收获青稞。上图左一为次仁拉姆 1961年

In 1961, a peasant named Tserin Lhamo from Gyebra Township, Shannan County organized 11 poorest nangtsen as a mutual aid group. They worked in the field and harvested.

次仁拉姆与丈夫过着幸福的生活 2009年

Tserin Lhamo and her husband living a happy life in 2009.

Chaida's House

Chaida is singing,
Sing for her childhood partners:
Broken jars and broken pans,
Empty baskets or the daydreams.

Hungry with empty stomach,
Wet in the rain,
Digging arrowroots with shaking hands and swollen feet.
Tears dropping into the soil then,
Tears dropping onto the glass table now.
The pictures on the wall is the witness,
Let me talk about the new home.

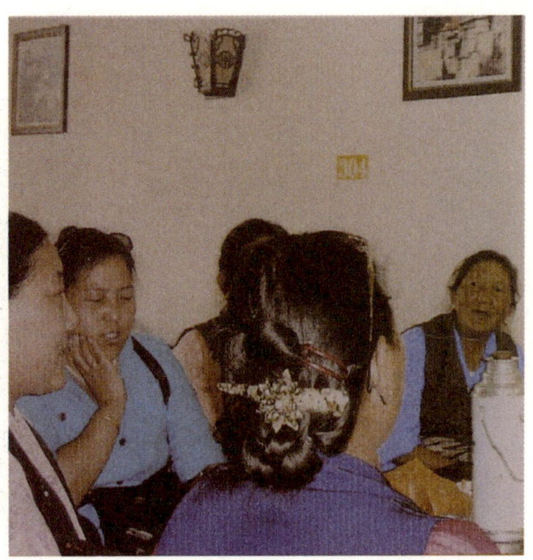

柴妲的家 1999年 Chaida's house in 1999.

柴妲的家

柴妲在唱歌，
唱她小时候的伴侣：
不是烂罐就是破锅，
不是空篓就是空梦。

饥肠断，
心如淖，
抖手肿脚挖苦葛*。
当年泪水落入泥，
如今泪水落到玻璃桌。
挂画为我做证，
新屋任我啰唆。

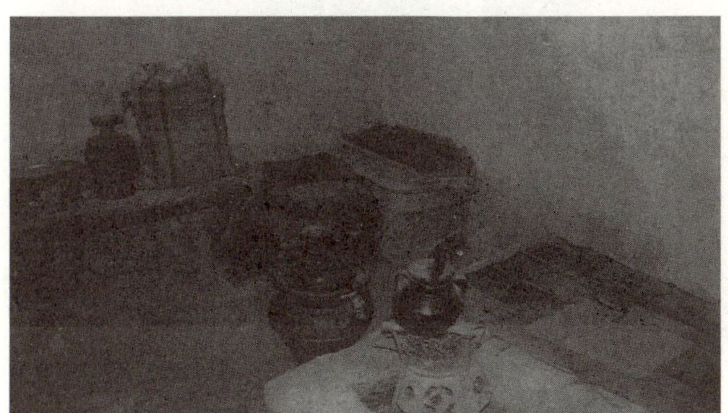

柴妲的家 20世纪50年代初 Chaida's house in the early 1950s.

*苦葛，一种根，苦涩，有淀粉。

*Arrowroots, a bitter root containing starch.

阿男家 *Anan's*

“堆穷”阿男一家7口人住在贵族的马棚里，每年以服“乌拉”差抵租 20世纪50年代初

Anan, a düjung serf, living in the barn of nobles with his family of 7 people. He paid his rent by offering free labor in the early 1950s.

阿男的家 2007年 Anan's house in 2007.

莫拉家 *Molha's*

莫拉家 20世纪50年代初

Molha's house in the early 1950s.

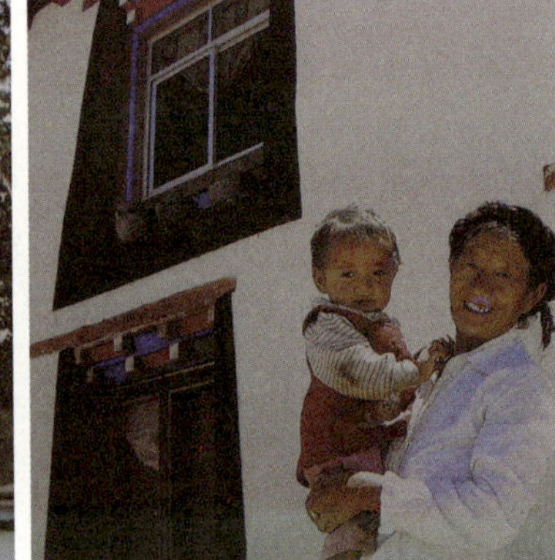

莫拉的家 2007年 Molha's house in 2007.

彭芭家 *Penpa's*

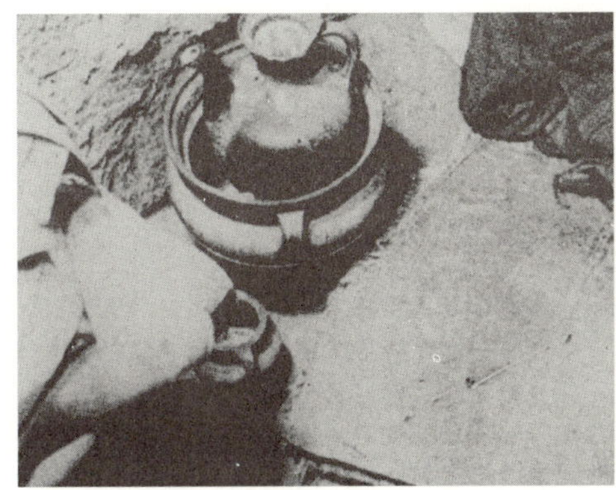

彭芭的家 20世纪50年代初
Penpa's house in the early 1950s.

彭芭的新家 2008年 Penpa's new house in 2008.

卓玛家 *Cholma's*

卓玛的家 1957年 Cholma's house in 1957.

卓玛的家 2007年 Cholma's house in 2007.

村舍 *Village Houses*

农奴居住的小屋 1950年以前

Serf's house before 1950.

拉萨贵族居住小楼 1956年

Lhasa noble residence in 1956.

拉萨的居民小区 1999年 Residential area in Lhasa in 1999.

拉萨的居民小区 2008年 Residential area in Lhasa in 2008.

第八章

蔚蔚人寰

Chapter 8 The World of Humans

雪莲冻开

如来如愿

观音关爱

Snow Lotus in Blossom

Wishes from Buddha

Love from Goddess of Mercy

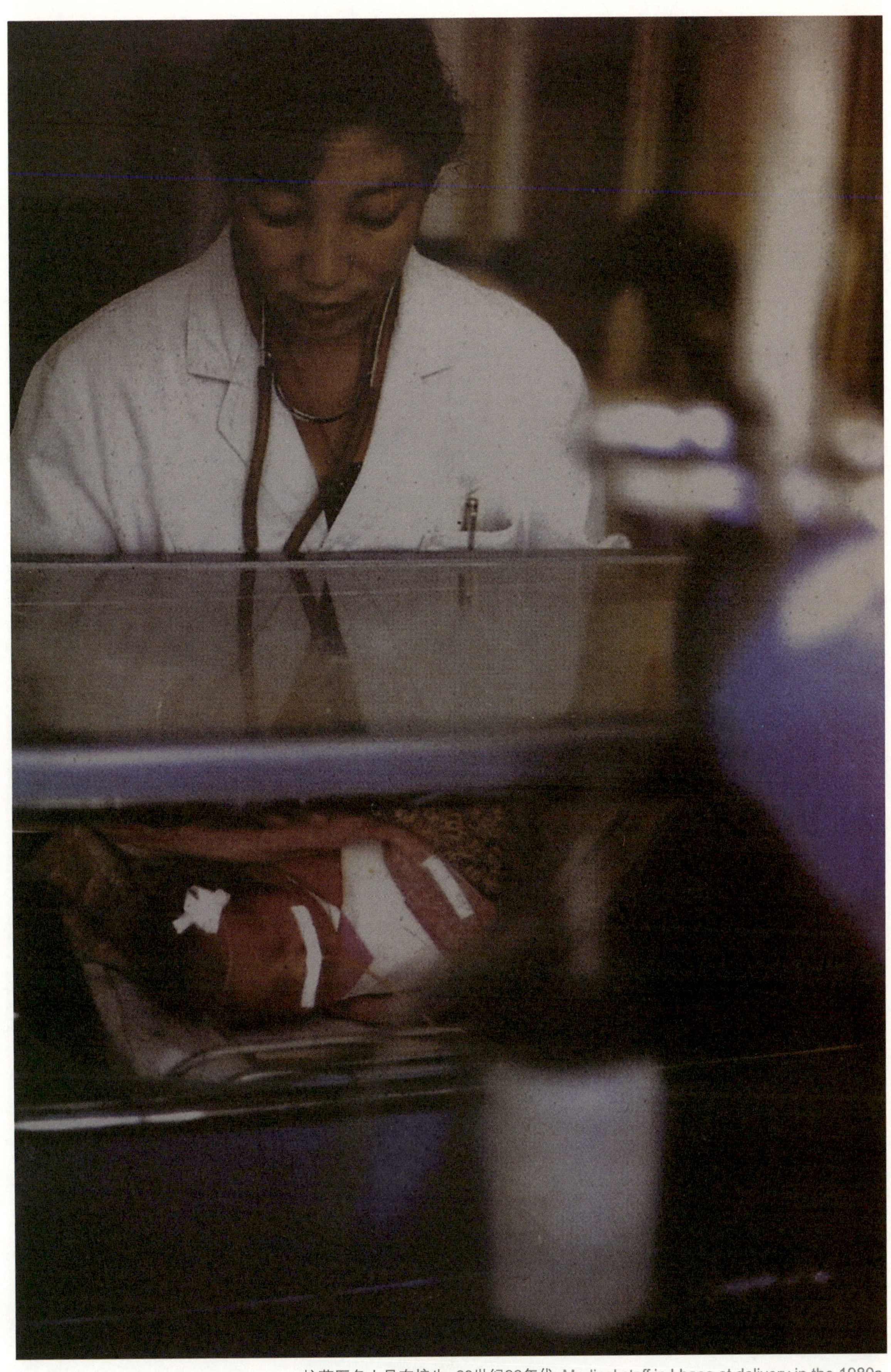

拉萨医务人员在接生 20世纪80年代 Medical staff in Lhasa at delivery in the 1980s.

牛粪堆 2007年 Cow dung heap in 2007.

牛粪上分娩，
生命不值钱。
雪对瘠地风云转，
暖阳出高原。

Laboring on cow dung,
Worthless in life.
Snowy highlands with stormy sky,
From the highlands coming warm sunshine.

农奴白天大部分时间必须下地干活，无法照料刚出生的婴儿，只能将孩子放在地头 20世纪50年代以前

The serfs had to work most of the day and could not care for their newborn babies, so they had to put the babies in the field before the 1950s.

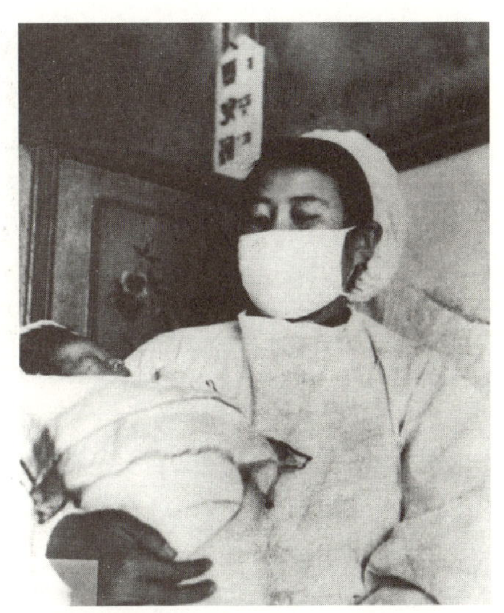

拉萨人民医院医务人员在接生 20世纪50年代

Medical staff of Lhasa People's Hospital at birth delivery in the 1950s.

观音本关爱，
如来就如愿。
蔚蔚人寰心为美，
茫茫雪海顿然安。
不过昆仑不识岭，
不到拉萨不震撼。

The Goddess of Mercy's love for all people,
The Tathagata Buddha's answer to all wishes.
All about the hearty feelings,
Travelling on the vast sea of snow.
Knowing not how high if having not climbed
over the Kunlun Mountain,
Knowing not how inspirational if having not visited Lhasa.

拉萨市妇幼保健院 2016年

Lhasa Women and Children Hospital in 2016.

英国人在拉萨德西林卡办的医院 1940年
British hospital in Dekyi Lingka in 1940.

拉萨街头的牙科诊所 2016年
Dental clinic on street of Lhasa in 2016.

拉萨市医院 2008年 Lhasa City Hospital in 2008.

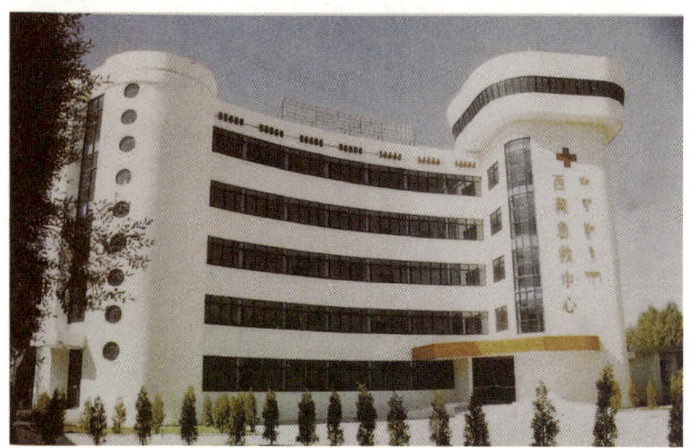

西藏急救中心 2008年
Hospital Emergency Center of Tibet in 2008.

西藏结核病控制中心 1999年
Tuberculosis Control Center of Tibet in1999.

An old bike, a medicine bag,

Travelling thousands of miles,

On this vast prairie,

You are seen everywhere.

Your face flushed with rosy cheeks,

Sweat-soaked clothes dried by winds.

Your medicine is the best,

Your youth setting the prairie afire,

Most gorgeous!

援藏汉族女医生 20世纪60年代

A Han female doctor in the Aid to Tibet Project in the 1960s.

一辆旧车，一个药包，

行万里，

浩瀚草原，

哪里都能见到你。

高地日晒红，

风干汗水衣。

你的药最好，

你的青春燎原，

最绚丽！

藏族老医生手把手传授医学知识 20世纪70年代

Old Tibetan doctor teaching medical knowledge in the 1970s.

Tibet is said to be the roughest,

I see Tibet to be the prettiest.

Paint pictures on snowfields,

Antiphonal on highlands,

To sing with windward.

Come here, dream catchers,

Go away, joy seekers!

人说西藏最艰巨，

我看西藏最绚丽。

雪海作画，

高山对诗，

长风当歌。

寻梦者，来，

求乐人，去！

藏药 *Tibetan medicine*

制作藏药药丸 1938年

Making Tibetan medicine pills in 1938.

藏医在牧区巡诊 1961年

Tibetan medicine doctor visiting pastoral areas in 1961.

手工作坊中的传统藏药生产 20世纪70年代

Tibetan medicine being made by hand in a workshop in the 1970s.

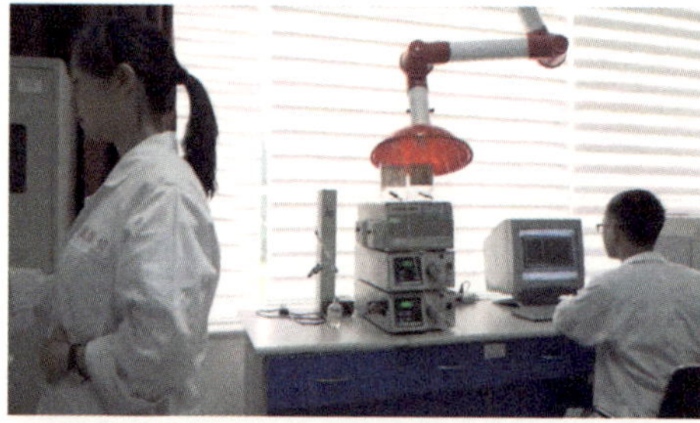

西藏第一家高新技术制药上市企业诺迪康，集藏药产品研发、生产和销售于一体 2016年

Nuodikang, the first high-tech pharmaceutical listed company in Tibet, integrating R&D, production and sales of Tibetan medicine products in 2016.

医学院 *Medical College*

西藏藏医学院成立于1989年，被誉为藏医学“医圣”“药王”的宇妥·云丹贡布的雕像矗立在教学楼前

Tibetan Traditional Medical College was founded in 1989, with a statue of “King of Tibetan Medicine” Yuthok Uden Gongbu standing in front of the school building.

顺利完成学业的西藏藏医学院毕业生 2014年

Graduates of Tibetan Traditional Medical College, who successfully completed their studies in 2014.

破产后带着孩子流浪的农奴 20世纪50年代初

A serf wandering with her child after bankruptcy in the early 1950s.

希望在人间，
不忘有从前。
与狗争食巴巴眼，
娃儿捆牢用绳牵。
高墙下，
庙堂边，
处处孤苦寒。

昔日流浪乞讨地，
今晨和风问早安。

Hopeful in the world,
Forget not the past.
For food fighting with dogs,
Boy tied with a rope.
At high walls,
By the temples,
Misery everywhere.

Where once the homeless begging,
Now where greeting morning.

西藏尼玛县小学生 2016年

Pupils from Nyima County in 2016.

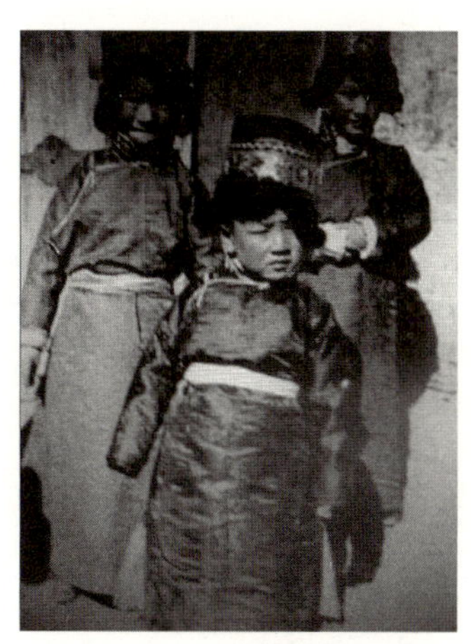

贵族子弟 1937年

Noble's children in 1937.

命运

少爷乐哈哈，
因为，他是我们的主人。
童儿泪涟涟，
因为，我们与他不是同一阶层。
同是人却两个样，
恰似庙里的鬼与神。

Fate

The young gentle is smiling with joy,
For he is our master.
The children are tearful,
For we are at the bottom under him.
We all have one life but of two kinds,
There are also ghosts with Buddhas in temple.

刚到德木活佛府上当侍从的农民噶曲（左）和格龙（右）约20世纪40年代

Gagqu (left) and Gelong (right) , two serfs when they first arrived in Demo Living Buddha's house to be attendants around the 1940s.

债 *Debt*

庄园管家向农奴收取初生婴儿的人头税 20世纪50年代初

A housekeeper of manor collecting head tax on newborn babies from serfs in the early 1950s.

在农奴等级制度下，农奴遭受一代又一代的剥削与压迫。农奴婴儿出生后，母亲必须抱着婴儿到管家那里按等级上报，成为新的农奴，并由其负责偿还父母前辈人所欠的债务。

Under the feudal-serf system, the serfs suffered from exploitation and oppression from generation to generation. When a serf's child was born, the mother had to take the baby to her owner's home to register and pay the birth-tax, since then the child became a personal belonging to his owner to repay the debt owed by his parents.

烧掉债据 1959年

Burning off the debt receipts in 1959.

孔繁森与他领养的藏族孤儿曲印和贡桑 1992年

Kong Fansen with his adopted Tibetan orphans Quin and Gongsang in 1992.

依偎阿爸身旁，
唱着歌儿惊货郎。
走大街，
逛小巷，
不用绳捆，不见娘。
啊！
原来不是他亲生，
是他路旁捡来由他养，
一把屎来一把尿，
稚声唤处有父影，
酣酣梦乡父伴旁。

Leaning against dad,
Brother's singing alerts vendors.
Walking on the street,
Roaming in the allies,
No ropes to tie, no view of the mother.
Ah!
Not his own bio-kids,
But his adopted kids,
Raised by dad,
Wherever a baby cries,
Sleeps deeply by dad.

农奴的孩子被父母拴在田间的木桩上 1957年

Serfs tying their children to a wood stick in the fields in 1957.

解	***Solution***
绳子不捆有人偷，	*Stolen if ropes not used to tie,*
寺规不严会开溜。	*People going wild if rules not strict in the temple.*
散学校铃响，	*At the bell of dismissal,*
快步向家走。	*Hurrying home.*

日喀则农村小学桑木小学的学生放学回家 20世纪80年代

Pupils from Sangmu Primary School, Shigatse going home after school in the 1980s.

贵族子弟 1952年 Noble's children in 1952.

不同脸膛不同笑，
苦乐喜愁天知道。
前世今生变世道，
踏实日子真可靠。

Different smiles on different faces,
Only Heaven knows misery and joy,
happiness and worries.
Past and present changes,
Peaceful days are reliable.

小小眼神多落寞，
似雷撼。
盼与望，
祈与愿。
欢声笑语不在言，
快乐就在我心间。

Little eyes look at your bosom,
Thundering shocking.
Expecting and longing,
Praying and wishing.
Too much happiness more than words,
But deep down in the hearts.

藏族小孩 2016年 Tibetan child in 2016.

放学归来的小学生 20世纪50年代末

Pupils coming home after school in the late 1950s.

带露的花儿
最美，
初升的太阳
最亮。

Flowers with dews on,
The most beautiful.
The rising sun,
The most brightest.

尼玛县小学做游戏的孩子们 2016年

Pupils from Nyima County playing games in 2016.

拉萨街头的流浪儿 1956年

Gutter children of Lhasa in 1956.

Yesterday, Today

How many children paupers,
How pitiful.
How many miseries,
How many nightmares of parents.

昨天，今天

多少流浪儿，
多少泪伶仃。
多少人间撕心事，
多少爹娘夜盼明。

尼玛县小学的小学生 2016年

Pupils from Nyima County in 2016.

农奴带着她的孩子在街头流浪乞讨 1957年

Serf begging in the street with her child in 1957.

阳光下青稞田里的孩子 20世纪90年代

Children in the Tibetan barley fields under the sun in the 1990s.

阳光

当年暴风雪来到，
妈妈拖着我们去乞讨。
而今丰收时刻，
妈妈带上我们
在金色的谷田里嬉笑。
知道不?
乞讨与嬉笑各是什么滋味?
乞讨，是心底的苦涩，
嬉笑，是春天的阳光。

Sunlight

In the past, when snowstorms came,
Mother took us to beg.
Nowadays, when the harvest time comes,
Mother takes us to the golden fields to laugh and play.
Do you know?
What it feels like to beg and to laugh and play?
To beg is bitterness at bottom of the heart,
To laugh and play is the spring sunlight.

牧民一家 1938年 A herdsmen family in 1938.

童颜

灰土地，泥巴里，
半只饭团难充饥。
虽俱去，
难忘记，
今昔对比，
感叹不已。

Baby Face

On the grey ground and in mud,
Still starving with a half rice ball.
Although gone are those days,
Yet unforgettable,
Comparing the past with the present,
Sighing and wondering unceasingly.

牧民家的两兄妹 2016年
Brother and sister of a herdsmen family in 2016.

西藏农奴带着孩子在街头流浪乞讨 20世纪中叶

Serf begging on the street with her child in the mid-20th century.

昔日的流浪儿，
今日的小学生。
一个万般无奈，
一个充满自信。
一个无精打采，
一个聚精会神。
世道真的变了，
一筐道理说不清。
说不清来就不说，
跟着太阳向前行。

A pauper to a pupil,
Helplessness to confidence,
Listlessness to concentration.
The world changed,
Too much to explain.
No need to explain;
Start a good journey following the sun.

藏族儿童在小学 20世纪70年代

Tibetan children studying in primary school in the 1970s.

岁月

板上脸，
木呆眼。
似疏，
又远。

扬起手，
笑开口。
阳光洒心头。

拉萨儿童 20世纪50年代初
Children of Lhasa in the early 1950s.

Years

Straight, long faces,
Fixed staring eyes.
Seemingly drifting,
And far as well.

Hands waving,
Laughing and smiling.
Filled with sunshine.

笑颜 2010年 Smile of Tibetan children in 2010.

抓小鸡

“老鹰抓小鸡”，
自古儿童戏。
同一宫墙黄原地，
换了“日托”*好稀奇！

好稀奇，
雪域处处“小鸡”嬉。
只不过，
人烟荒芜难寻迹。

Playing snatching chicks

"Eagles snatching chicks",
Played by kids since ancient times.
A scene of desolation outside the same palace walls,
How strange now a "daycare"!*

Not strange,
Chicks playing everywhere in the snowland.
Only,
Their traces are hard to find in the wilderness.

老师和孩子们做游戏 20世纪50年代末

Kindergarten teachers playing games with children in the late 1950s.

幼儿园老师带着孩子们做游戏 2007年

Kindergarten teachers playing games with children in 2007.

*日托，白天托管幼儿的服务，由法定监护人以外的人来照看。

*Daycare is the care of a child during the day by a person other than the child's legal guardians.

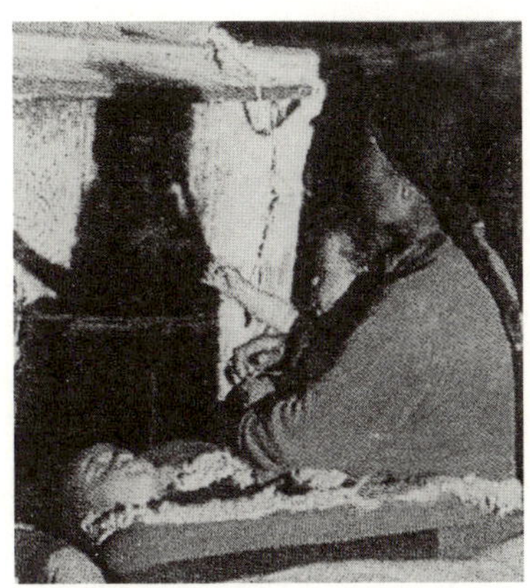

农妇和她的孩子 20世纪50年代初

A serf and her child in the early 1950s.

搬进新家的拉萨居民 2007年

Lhasa residents moving into their new home in 2007.

People of Lhasa

Expecting,
Pointing to the small god stove,
My shadow that is.
I want to be a god,
Sitting in and doing nothing every day,
Face unwashed, but still respected.

Expecting,
Pointing to the top of the Potala Palace,
Picturesque Lhasa it is!
Better views on the higher position,
Beautiful snow scenes.
God's stove is not so beautiful as Lhasa,
Being a god is not as good as being a citizen of Lhasa.

拉萨人

指望，
在矮小的神灶前指望，
那是我的影子。
我要成神，
成天坐着不做事，
不洗脸，有人敬。

指望，
在布宫顶上指望，
那是如画的拉萨！
高处看得清，
雪域好风景。
神灶哪有拉萨美，
做神不如做拉萨人。

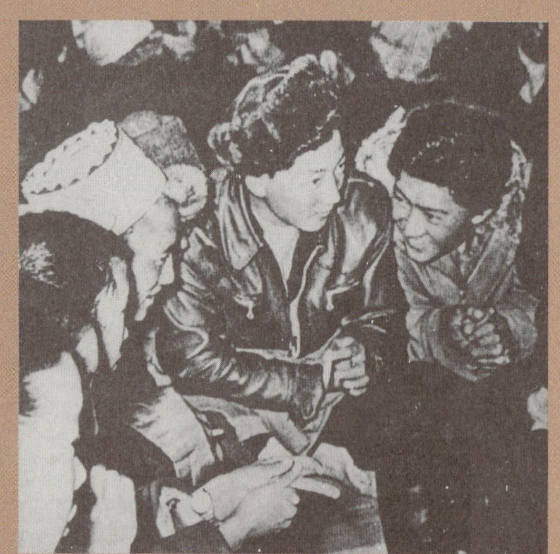

1959年，中国国务院发布命令解散原西藏地方政府，由西藏自治区筹备委员会行使西藏地方政府职权，拉萨市各族青年欢欣鼓舞地讨论着国务院的命令。

In 1959, the State Council of PRC issued an order to dissolve the former Tibetan local government. The Tibet Autonomous Region preparatory committee executed the power of the Tibetan local government. The young people of all ethnic groups in Lhasa discussing the State Council's order delightfully.

牧场上的骏马与少年 20世纪90年代

A horse and a young man in a ranch in the 1990s.

牦牛队

跨上牦牛背，
潇洒走一回。
男人赶牛乱成团，
看我轻去快归。

运盐的牦牛队 1956年
Yak teams carrying salt bags in 1956.

A Yak Team

On yaks' back,
Travelling around.
Yaks were driven into confusion by males,
Let me drive yaks home with ease and speed.

雪中牦牛队 2006年 Yak teams in snow in 2006.

西藏山南乃东的牧马人 1938年

A wrangler from Nêdong County, Shannan in 1938.

骏马帅少年，
驾车行路远。
汽车跑过马，
一年新一年。
高原盛事多哟！
雪海深邃处，
今夏竞舷帆。

Steed and handsome youth,
Driving a further distance.
Autos faster than horses,
Each year better than the last one.
New things appear on highlands!
On the deep sea of snow,
Sailing races this summer.

开大货车的藏族司机 20世纪90年代

A Tibetan driver driving a truck in the 1990s.

旧西藏铁匠地位很低，没有资格把碗放在别人家的桌子上 1921年

Tibetan blacksmiths had very low social status in the past and were not allowed to put bowls on the tables in 1921.

假日里拉萨市的女工换上新装，到绿树成荫的雪策林卡里游玩 1959年

Female workers in Lhasa putting on new clothes on holiday and playing in Shötro Lingka in 1959.

彩裙之诉

选美先下看，
倩女先倩裙。
裙风扫尽英雄汉，
裙下倾国又倾城。

The Tale of Color Skirts

Beauty pageant, first looking down,
Selecting pretty girls by their beautiful skirts.
All heroes in homage of gorgeous skirts,
Lovely enough to cause the fall of a state.

五彩斑斓的藏族服饰 2010年 Colorful Tibetan costumes in 2010.

牧羊女

在所有的旷野中，
最不定的是我的草原。
在所有的珍藏中，
最好看的都挂在我的腰间。
在所有的娇媚中，
最美丽的是牧羊女的笑脸。

藏族女牧民 1938年

A Tibetan female herdsman in 1938.

Shepherdess

All over the wilderness,
The least settled is my prairie.
Of all treasures,
The most beautiful are all hung around my waist.
Of all the beauties,
The prettiest are the smiles on the shepherdesses' face.

聂荣县尼玛乡的牧羊女 2007年

A shepherdess from Nyima Township, Nyainrong County in 2007.

拉萨郊外的浣衣女 1957年

A woman washing clothes on the outskirts of Lhasa in 1957.

百媚

一副笑盈满，
一双眼望穿。
花枝花儿初放，
妩媚冰山雪莲。

养路女工 20世纪90年代

Female road maintenance workers in the 1990s.

Cute Beauties

A smiling face,
A pair of longing eyes.
Flower just blossoming,
Charming iceberg snow lotus.

来自牧区的夫妻 1938年

A couple from the pastoral area in 1938.

色季拉山区高原牧场上的一对夫妻 20世纪60年代

A couple on a highland pasture in Sejira Mountain in the 1960s.

情侣

我有情来你有意，

蜂儿沾上蜜。

不在车来不在衣，

天堂，地狱，

跟定了，

随君去。

Lovers

My love and your love,

Bees on honey.

Careless about cars and clothes,

Heaven or hell,

For sure,

I follow you.

藏族小伙子为姑娘弹奏吉他 1999年

A Tibetan lad playing the guitar for girls in 1999.

姐妹花

雪城草原花，
如画更胜画。
岁月知多少，
相看竞风华。

察隅少女吹牧笛 1956年

Girls from Zayü blowing flute in 1956.

Sisters

Grass flowers of the snow city,
Like paintings, only better.
How much time passed,
How beautiful it looks.

门巴女子 1997年 Monpa women in 1997.

草原姐妹花 2016年 Sisters on green meadow in 2016 .

朵朵姐妹花，
苦乐哀愁全在画。
入寺当尼出家，
一身破衣烂片。
入读大学拉萨，
一色红锦彩缎。
时代不由你和我，
幸有今日手牵。

藏族女性 1903年 Tibetan women in 1903.

藏族姐妹花 1981年 Tibetan sisters in 1981.

Sisters are like flowers,
Happiness and bitterness are all in the painting.
Becoming nuns in temples,
In the same rags.
Going to college in Lhasa.
In the same crimson silk.
You and I can't control the time,
We are fortunate today to be hand in hand.

拉萨街头骑自行车的藏族女孩 1999年
Tibetan girls riding bicycles on the streets in Lhasa in 1999.

第九章

初阳旋律

Chapter 9 The Melody of Newborn Sun

学府
育人
书市
藏文

Higher Education
Education
Book Markets
Tibetan Language

拉萨小学生 2004年 Pupils of Lhasa in 2004.

“现在西藏有81%的儿童受过教育，而这在那受到赞美的传统时代只有2%。”
——法国埃松省参议员梅朗雄

"There are 81% of children educated in Tibet, which compared to that old era by praise, only 2% of children enter the classroom."
——Senator Jean-Luc Melenchon (Essonne Province, France)

拉萨的大街 1938年 The main street of Lhasa in 1938.

全城商店无藏名，	*Shops in the city had no shop signs in Tibetan language,*
全城街路无藏文。	*Streets had no Tibetan signage for their names.*
全城不卖书与报，	*Bookstores and newspaper stands were not around,*
名曰“圣城”实盲城。	*So called "The Holy City" is actually the city of illiteracy.*

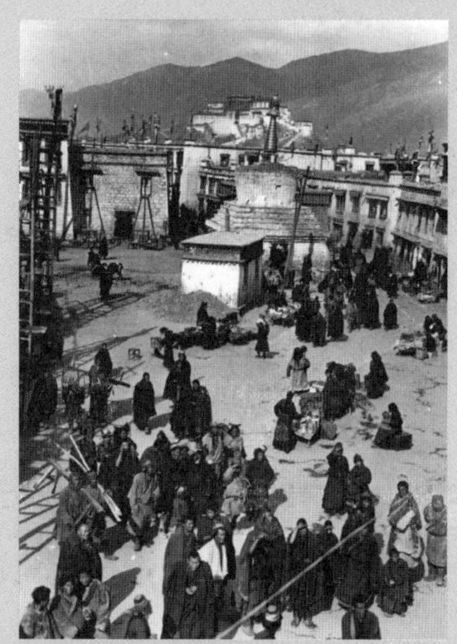

拉萨的大街 1938年

The main street of Lhasa in 1938.

从难见藏文的“盲城”到满目藏文的文灿之都

1959年十四世达赖喇嘛南逃印度后，有关西藏情况的报道，西方媒体一直是负面的。这些报道为十四世达赖喇嘛主政西藏地方政权前后时期（包括1960年前）的“达赖文化”叫好。

但是，事实真是如此吗?

笔者在20世纪50年代初进藏时，并没有“达赖文化”的说法。下面的照片和诗歌，反映了20世纪50年代前后西藏老百姓生活的巨大变化。

20世纪50年代初，拉萨的商店没有藏文招牌，街道没有藏文的路牌，房屋没有藏文的门牌，甚至主管拉萨政务的市政厅前也没有藏文的招牌或公告牌。加上没有书店，没有报摊，没有公立学校，只有贵族子弟上的私塾，全城很难看到藏文，俨然是一个缺少文字的盲城。

The western media has been especially negative on Tibet reports since the 14th Dalai Lama ran off to India in 1959. They usually applaud for the period of time when Dalai Lama and his government was in power including the time before 1960.

But are those times really the best years of Tibet?

When I went to Tibet in the 1950s there was no such thing as "Dalai Culture". The following pictures and poems show the changes of people in Tibetan before and after the 1950s.

In the beginning of the 1950s, business shops in Lhasa had no shop signs in Tibetan language, streets had no Tibetan signboards, houses had no Tibetan number plates, and the city hall had no Tibetan signboard or notice board. There were also no bookstores or newsstands. There were no public schools, and only a few children from aristocratic families had chance to attend private schools. In the city one can barely see any Tibetan language writings, and some said that it was a city of illiteracy.

拉萨的大街 1938年 The main street of Lhasa in 1938.

官贵过市大众闪两旁，
洋贵上街平民惊两厢。
贵骄民困一幕幕，
“达赖文化”正登场。
正登场，
拉萨上空灰茫茫，
无文无字锁城乡。
世道何横，
人心何惶。

When dignitaries passed the street,
People gave away to them from afar.
The local grandees were proud while people humble,
Was a true portrayal of "Dalai's Lhasa".
Illiteracy locks cities and countryside.
Time was hard,
People strive to reach nirvana with moral stamina.
Society was not equal ,
People were not calm.

权贵过处平民闪到两旁 1900年左右

The civilians making way for the nobles around 1900.

八廓街的商店店招 2015年

Shop signs of the Barkhor Street in 2015.

拉萨街上抬头看，
藏文花枝招展，
汉文正正端端。
藏在上，
汉在下，
“大汉” 作“小汉”。

Watching in the streets of Lhasa,
Tibetan words are gorgeously dressed.
Chinese words are square and regular.
The Tibetan ones written above,
The Chinese ones written below,
So shown respect,
By changing "Great Han" into "Small Han".

据统计，西藏自治区藏族人口达三百多万，拉萨定期公开出版的藏文报刊有:

11种藏文报纸

14种藏文杂志

42个24小时藏语频道

可笑的是，“藏独”和西方主流媒体却长期指斥中国要“消灭”藏文、藏语和藏文化，要禁止“信仰自由”。

这正是：

叛祖忘典地骂承传，
停滞倒退地骂发展。
滑天下之大稽，
笑破胆，
举世叹!

阅读《西藏日报》的牧民 1957年

Tibetan herdsmen reading *Tibet Daily* in 1957.

Tibet has a population over 3 million. Now there are 11 kinds of Tibetan newspaper, 14 kinds of Tibetan magazines and 42 Tibetan television channels broadcasting 24 hours a day.

These facts show how ridiculous that those who support “Tibet independence” reproach China for “eliminating” Tibetan language and culture and “forbidding” freedom of religion.

It exactly is:
Ones who betrayal of the ancestors abuse ones who inheriting,
Ones who standstill and retrograde abuse ones who developing.
Be the biggest joke in the world,
Make a great laughingstock of,
And all the world wondering.

书市

八廓街上的经书摊 1938年

Scripture stalls on the Barkhor Street in 1938.

虽说“书市”
又无书来又没市。
经片摊子地上摆，
经片风中飞扬。
百姓人家不识字，
何须书和市！

Although a "book market",
No books nor customers.
Scripture pieces displayed on the ground,
Scripture pieces flying with the wind.
The illiterate can't write or read,
Book markets weren't needed!

拉萨市新华书店 2007年 Xinhua Bookstore of Lhasa in 2007.

据西藏文史资料记载，和平解放之前，西藏有寺院教育、官办教育和私塾教育三种教育形式。全西藏有70余所官办教育学校，以学习藏语文、数学、藏医学等为主，通常是上层贵族、官员的子女就读；私塾学校有80余所，以学习藏语文为主，这些学校在校学生人数极少，且没有明确的学制规定；在寺院，则是只有具有一定地位、级别的僧人才能接受文化教育。

旧西藏没有新型的近代学校教育，广大农牧民子女没有人身自由，更谈不上有受教育的机会。这些直接导致旧西藏文盲率高达95%以上。

According to Tibetan historical records, before the Peaceful Liberation, Tibet had three types of education: monastic education, government-runned education and private-school education. There were about 70 government-runned educational schools in Tibet that mainly taught Tibetan, Mathematics and Tibetan medicine, usually for the children of upper aristocrats and officials. There were about 80 private schools that mainly taught Tibetan, the number of students in the school was very small, and there was no clear academic rules. In the monastery there was a certain status for the level of monks to receive cultural and education.

There were no new type of modern school education in old Tibet, and the majority of children of peasants and herdsmen had no freedom, not to mention the chance of receiving education. These directly led to the illiteracy rate in old Tibet as high as 95%.

拉萨小学生扎西央宗帮妈妈学习基础读写 20世纪50年代初

Lhasa pupil Drashi Yangdzom helping her mother study basic reading and writing in the early 1950s.

八廓街上的经书摊 20世纪50年代初

Scripture stalls on the Barkhor Street in the early 1950s.

世道真沧桑，
书屋书楼竞比高。
经片摊子变成了经书店，
“多种经书店”，
五个大字多耀眼。
文盲拉萨城，
已是往昔事，
说“再见”！

八廓街上的多种经书店 1999年

Bookstore of various scriptures on the Barkhor Street in 1999.

Time indeed changed,
More and more bookstores.
Scripture piece venders turned into
scripture bookstores,
“Bookstore of Various Scriptures”
Five glittering words.
Illiterate Lhasa,
Long gone,
Say “Good-bye”!

无书不西藏，
拉萨飘书香。
前世佛陀殿，
今日诗书长。

Without book there is no Tibet,
Without book there is no Lhasa.
After kowtowing in the Buddha temple,
They immerse themselves in books to discover.

拉萨新华书店中的读书人 2006年

Readers in the Xinhua Bookstore of Lhasa in 2006.

从前拉萨无书卖，
现在拉萨有书街。
识文断字耳目聪，
书香拉萨飘中外。

Lhasa had no bookstores before,
but now it has a street of bookstores.
Lhasa is no longer an illiterate city,
Scholarly Lhasa is world renowned.

学经的小僧侣 20世纪40年代

A little monk studying scripture in the 1940s.

No public schools, but there are old private schools,

Pupils accompanied by whip and board,

One to hit pupils with,

One to write on.

Only one book of Buddhism to be read till broken and torn.

没有学校有私塾，

鞭板各一伴读书，

一条打人的鞭子，

一块写字的板子。

一本经书读到烂。

日喀则私塾的教师在批改学生书法作业 1957年

A teacher from a private school in Shigatse correcting students' calligraphy work in 1957.

日喀则郊区私塾的学生向塾师呈交藏文书法作业 1957年

A student from a private school in the suburbs of Shigatse handing in his calligraphy work to his teacher in 1957.

藏族女学生 2007年 Tibetan schoolgirls in 2007.

学校食堂用餐 2007年 Dining in the school canteen in 2007.

公学，
小学，
中学，
大学，
学校一个接一个，
学生几十到几万。
全城琅琅读书声，
别了，
拉萨儿童流浪城。

练习藏文的小学生 20世纪50年代中期 Pupils practicing Tibetan calligraphy in the mid-1950s.

藏族小学生 1987年 Tibetan pupils in 1987.

Public schools,
Primary schools,
Middle schools,
Universities,
School after school,
Students from dozens to tens of thousands.
Reading sounds all over the city,
Good-bye!
Lhasa, the city of paupers.

拉萨第三小学开学，兴高采烈的孩子们 1959年

Delightful children on the opening ceremony of the Lhasa No. 3 Primary School in 1959.

校门开得早，　*The school gate is open early,*
迎接学生到，　*Welcoming my kids,*
书香满教室，　*The classroom is full of fragrance of books,*
书开满脸笑。　*Books open and smile on faces.*

读书的藏族儿童 2016年 Tibetan children reading books in 2016.

一支笔儿比天长，	*A pencil long enough to reach the sky,*
一翻课本跨过江。	*Opening the book would take you across the river.*
书中自有天外天，	*Heavens beyond heaven in the book,*
字字伴艳阳。	*Every character with its brilliance.*
居室哪能比课堂，	*Bedrooms have no comparison to classrooms,*
女妆哪能比诗章。	*Make-ups have no comparison to poems.*
琅琅书声起，	*Here comes the reading sound,*
你也娇来她更靓。	*Charming are you and lovely is she.*

藏族小学生 1981年 Tibetan pupils in 1981.

农牧区的孩子和大人在接受教育 20世纪50年代初

Children and adults in agricultural and pastoral areas receiving education in the early 1950s.

骑自行车的藏族小学生 2007年 Tibetan pupils riding bicycles to school in 2007.

一些牧民在扫盲，
一群孩子在歌唱，
一堆儿女，
听妈妈把童话讲：
王子飞上了天空……
我不要当王，也不要做神，
只要有一辆新车伴我把学上。

Some herdsmen learning to read and write,
Singing are a group of children,
A bunch of kids,
Listening to their mother tell stories:
A handsome prince flies to heaven...
I don't want to be a king, nor to become a god,
Only to have a new bike to take me to school.

江孜英文学校教室 1923—1926年

A classroom in an English school at Gyantse around 1923—1926.

一间单房秃坡下，
几个丁点排成行。
洋帽洋礼称作“洋”，
又笑杀多少师长！

A hatch-roofed room at the footslope,
All petite in rows.
Western hats and rituals and foreign manners,
At ridiculous look teachers laughing heads off!

三名身穿西装的仁波切在热振活佛位于拉萨的别墅里 20世纪40年代

Three Rinpoche wearing suits in a villa in Lhasa of Reting Rinpoche in the 1940s.

江孜贵族学校由英国人于1923年创办。1927年，学校因英国教师被十三世达赖喇嘛驱逐而停办。1930年西藏地方政府任命藏人为校长、老师，学校复课，学生不到30人（学校只有一个班，不论年龄大小，学生均在同一班上课）。

Gyantse Noble School was established in 1923 by the British. In 1927 the school was closed as a result of the expulsion of the British teachers by the 13th Dalai Lama. In 1930, the Tibetan government appointed Tibetans to be the principal and teachers and reopened the school (There was only one class with students of all ages) with no more than 30 students.

江孜英文学校教室 1923—1926年 English school at Gyantse around 1923—1926.

第一所英语训练班，由十三世达赖喇嘛于1923年开办于江孜，用于培训军官和政府文职人员，每期有10—20人。

1924年，因英国人涉足藏军的政变，达赖于1927年下令关闭该训练班。

第二所英语训练班，由摄政王达扎活佛为加强与英国人的关系于1943年开办于拉萨。四个月后，由于寺庙的反对而停办。

1970年以后，因发展的需要和电脑的普及，英语被列入中学课程，拉萨许多人都在学英语。

The first English training class was set up by the 13th Dalai Lama in Gyantse in 1923 to train military officers and civilian officers, with 10-20 students in each.

In 1924, the class was ordered to close by the 13th Dalai Lama because the British was involved in the coup by the Tibetan Army.

The second English training class was set up by the Prince Regent in Lhasa in 1943 to strengthen relationships with the British. The class stopped four months later due to the opposition by the Buddhist temples.

Since the 1970s, with the development of tourism and wide use of computers, English has been a subject in the curriculum for middle schools, and most people in Lhasa have been learning English.

学习英语 2007年 Studying English in 2007.

留学生 *Oversea students*

西藏历史上第一位留学生擦珠·阿旺洛桑去日本留学 1911年 Cadrup Ngawang Lobsang, the first oversea student in Tibetan history went to Japan in 1911.

龙厦和四名学生在留英前合影 1914年 Lungshar and the four Tibetan students just before leaving for England in 1914.

外国学生在拉萨学习 20世纪80年代 Foreign students studying in Lhasa in the 1980s.

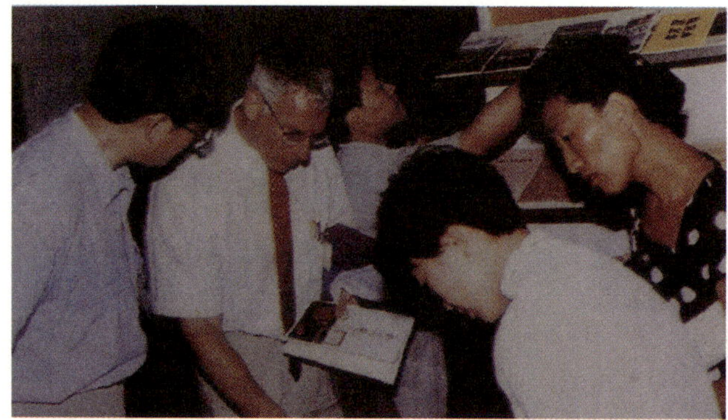

西藏大学和挪威几所大学进行了人才培养、学者互访等合作 20世纪90年代 Tibet University and several Norwegian universities carrying out a series of co-operation including talent development and mutual visits of scholars in the 1990s.

西藏历史上第一个自学考试的藏文成人教育培训班开学 1986年

The first self-study exam training course of adult Tibetan education in Tibetan history was started in 1986.

结束课程离开培训中心的学生 1999年

Students leaving the training center after finishing their training course in 1999.

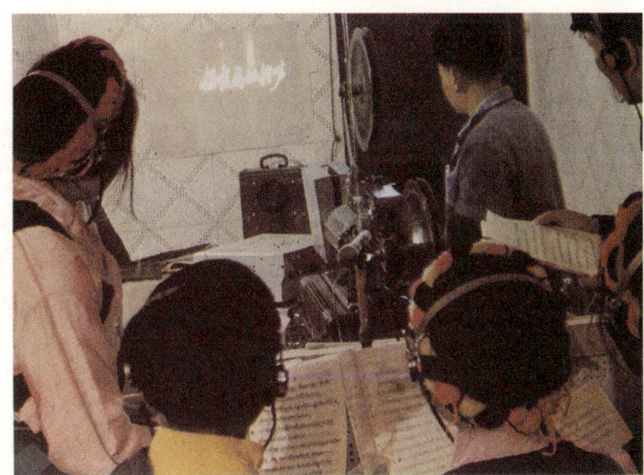

西藏自治区电化教育馆内的电影课 1999年

A film lesson in the Audio-Visual Education Hall of the Tibet Autonomous Region in 1999.

藏族老奶奶送孙子上西藏大学 2007年

A Tibetan old granny sending her grandson to the Tibet University in 2007.

许多哈达挂满身，
顶着奶奶的额头道一声：
“亲奶奶，我去了，
留下我的心。”

A lot of khatags put up,
Kissing grandmother's head, and saying
"I have to go, my dear grandma,
Let me leave my heart with you."

西藏农牧学院 2007年 Tibet Agricultural and Animal Husbandry College in 2007.

大学毕业生，
雪映人最美。
课堂新知识，
高原用不尽。
天这边独蓝，
情这边最深。

A college graduate,
So beautiful in snow's reflection.
Armed with new knowledge,
Applicable in the highlands.
So blue the sky here,
So magnificent the sentiments.

支教女教师和藏族小学生 2007年 A female volunteer teacher with Tibetan pupils in 2007.

第十章

高原风

Chapter 10 Trend of Highland

热情的西藏民间舞 2004年 Passionate Tibetan dance in 2004.

唱歌的儿童 1938年 Children singing songs in 1938.

一支乡曲，使你彷徨。
一首情歌，让君不忘。
乡曲、情歌，
不论由谁谱，由谁赋，
都要借我的眉来传情，
我的嗓子唱。

A country song makes you hesitate.
A love song makes it unforgetable.
Country songs and love songs,
Whoever the music composer and lyric writer,
All need to borrow my eyebrows to express emotions,
Borrow my voice to sing.

这是20世纪50年代初拉萨的一位歌女，年约16，岁月在她脸上留下的是中年女子的痕迹，使她显得过老。那时候拉萨的官贵把歌女看成是妓女，她们处于社会的最底层，是连寺院都不能进的人。

This was a female singer in Lhasa in the early 1950s. She was 16 years old, but time had left traces of adulthood on her face. At that time, officials and dignitaries in Lhasa treated female singers as a kind of prostitute who lived at the bottom of the society and could not go into any monasteries.

山沟里唱，
林子里合。
有谁来听？
空空一只讨钱盒。

你我都穷，
大家都饿。
有谁来听？
卖唱人凄凄，
荒野何蹉跎。

在拉萨德西林卡，一群来自康区的流浪艺人正在为英国人表演 1936年冬

Khampa dancers performing for the British Mission in Dekyi Lingka, Lhasa in winter of 1936.

在帐篷前演唱音乐的卖唱母女 1938年

Mother and daughter busking in front their tent in 1938.

They were in the valleys singing for living,
They were in the woods performing for surviving.
Who had the spare time for listening?
The change box was still empty.

You were poor; I was poor,
Everybody was on the edge of starving.
Who had the spare time for listening?
The singers were gloomy and helpless.
What a waste in the wilderness.

走过了
一千年的闭塞，
几世纪的沉锁。
告别了
关在酒楼里的小曲，
封在雪山沟的吆喝。

今已是
一唱雅江过，
再唱渡辽河。
十三亿人大合唱，
世界之最，
世界之歌。

Having walked
One thousand-year closure,
Centuries of blockage.
Having said farewell
To ditties sung in restaurants,
And shouts in the snowy valley.

Today the song is sung across
Yarlung Zangpo River first,
And Liaohe River next,
Echoed by 1.3 billion people in unity.
The greatest song of all over the world,
And the song is sung across all over the world.

一群流浪的琴手脚上戴着脚镣演奏 1921年

A group of itinerant fiddlers with shackles on their legs in 1921.

才旦卓玛出演大型舞蹈音乐史诗《东方红》 1964年

In 1964, Tseten Cholma starring in the musical epic *The East Is Red*.

韩红高歌，
汉藏亿万来合。
拂过一山又一山，
情染昆仑两翼乐。
起咏曲水，
领唱长江黄河。
牵起手来大合唱，
爱倾千城再倾国。

Han Hong is enthusiasticly singing,
Millions of Hans and Tibetans are chorusing.
The melody travels across Kunlun Mountain.
Ridges and ridges of mountains are echoing.
Joining hands people are singing
For love and the country's well-being.

我们吹奏大家和，
一歌唱罢又一歌。
藏歌首首响中天，
前倾山河后倾国。

来自巴塘的弦子琴 1995年 Tibetan folk art "Batang Xianzi" in 1995.

We are playing the Tibetan strings,
People are echoing.
All Tibetan songs are pleasant to Chinese,
All Chinese people think them fascinating.

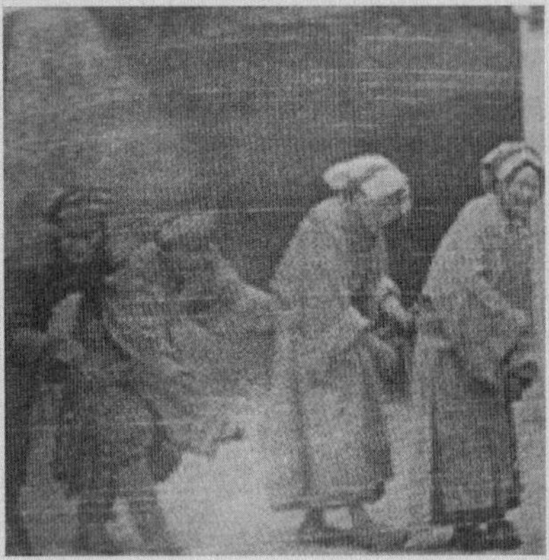

藏舞 20世纪50年代初
Tibetan dance in the early 1950s.

这个是舞?
不像。
是在捉迷藏?
也不像，
却又有几分凄凉。

这才是舞蹈，
哟!
手扬歌声飘，
裙风一阵起，
送君入梦乡。

藏舞 20世纪60年代初
Tibetan dance in the early 1960s.

Is it dance?
Not seems like.
Hide-and-seek?
Neither,
Somewhat miserable.

This is dance,
Wow!
Dancing to the songs,
Stirred up are the skirts,
Sending you to dreams.

西藏广场舞 2014年 Tibetan square-dancing in 2014.

自从中国兴起广场舞，西藏舞像风一样吹遍中国所有的城镇。每天有数百万人走入广场舞群，每个舞群几乎每晚都要播放西藏舞曲。

西藏广场舞有多种舞曲，广受欢迎，如《最美西藏》《想西藏》等。

Since the special Chinese square-dancing got popular in many cities and towns in China, Tibetan dancing style became well-spread too. Everyday millions of people in China participate in square-dancing and Tibetan dancing is seen on almost every square.

There are a variety of Tibetan dance music that people enjoy, such as *The Most Beautiful Tibet* and *Tibetan Memory*.

庆祝藏历新年的舞蹈 1938年
Dancing on Losar (Tibetan New Year) celebration in 1938.

大型民族音乐会上的藏舞 2010年 Tibetan dance on a large ethnic concert in 2010.

跳的是西藏舞步，
伴的是西藏舞曲。
踩的是山川大地，
震天擂鼓亿万一。
东起上海京津，
西迄新疆甘肃。
南自万泉珠江，
北至绥芬鸭绿。
点不完的广场空旷，
数不清的阿妈阿叔。
歌迎晨晓，
舞送日暮。
抛袖舞姿天下健，
扎西德勒华夏舒。

Dancing in Tibetan style,
Accompanying with Tibetan songs.
Stepping on the land of mountains and rivers,
Billions of people making a shocking pace.
East from Shanghai, Beijing and Tianjin,
West from Xinjiang and Gansu.
South from the Wanquanhe River and Zhujiang River,
North from the Suifenhe River and Yalu River.
Endless Tibetan square dances,
Singing before daybreak,
Dancing until sunset.
The world changing through Tibetan long-sleeve dancing,
With a Tashidler blessing Chinese people smiling.

上海杨浦中学的学生编排藏舞《北京的金山上》1975年

In 1975, students of Shanghai Yangpu Middle School setting choreography Tibetan dance *On the Golden Mountain of Beijing.*

舞蹈《溜溜康定溜溜的情》2012年 Dance *Kang Ding Qing* in 2012.

藏戏戏班觉木隆在罗布林卡上演《文成公主》 20世纪50年代末

Traditional Tibetan troupe Kyomulung performing *Princess Wencheng* in Norbulingka in the late 1950s.

布达拉宫德阳夏广场上演跳神"羌姆" 20世纪50年代末

Cham dancing on the Deyangshar courtyard of the Potala in the late 1950s.

各具特色的藏戏面具 20世纪50年代末 A variety of unique Tibetan drama masks in the late 1950s.

大型现代舞剧《红河谷》21世纪初 The large modern dance drama *Red River Valley* at the beginning of the 21th century.

说唱艺人在说唱《格萨尔王传》 20世纪50年代初

Narrator narrating *Epic of King Gesar* in the early 1950s.

地上一只讨饭碗，	*One bowl on the ground for begging,*
衬着两个说唱脸。	*Two faces roles of the play with talking and singing.*
白脸唱起来，	*White one singing in tune,*
灰脸打竹板。	*Grey one playing bamboo clappers.*

1981年，西藏大学格萨尔抢救小组正在录制著名格萨尔说唱艺人扎巴（中）的作品。扎巴能演唱数百万诗行的格萨尔史诗，被誉为“国宝”。

In 1981, members of Gesar rescue team from Tibet University recording famous narrator Zarba's works. Zarba could sing millions of poems in the *Epic of King Gesar*, and he is known as the “National Treasure”.

《格萨尔王传》*Epic of King Gesar*

在20世纪之前，格萨尔王的故事就已在西藏民间口口相传，也有小本章节的片段木刻版传。但从来没有人知道它有多少版本、多少章节、有多长。

格萨尔生于公元1038年，1054年为王，1119年殁，是西藏历史上最有影响的人物之一。

在20世纪50年代前，虽然世界高速发展，西藏地方政府却仍只注重当政者的权利，不曾对西藏历史上有巨大影响的重要文献进行收集。

20世纪80年代后期，中央人民政府决定把《格萨尔王传》列为重要社科项目，由中国社科院民族文学所和国家出版基金办公室牵头，组成上百人的采访小组，开始对在各地流传的《格萨尔王传》进行地毯式的收集和整理。经过长达十多年的工作，已整理出大体完整的格萨尔王长篇史诗，计120本、100多万行，2,000万字，并出版发行，《格萨尔王传》成为全世界最长的史诗。

Before the 20th century, the *Epic of King Gesar* had been circulating from mouth to mouth in Tibet. There were also legends of King Gesar carved in woodcut. No one ever knew how many versions and how many chapters it had, nor how long it was.

The King Gesar was born in 1038, crowned in 1054 and passed away in 1119. He was one of the most significant persons in Tibet.

Before the 1950s, knowing the high-speed development of the world, the Tibetan local government still only paid its attention to the rights of the persons in power. They did nothing in collecting important historical documents on matters that were once a great contribution to society.

In the late 1980s, the Central People's Government included "King Gesar" as an important social science project. The Ethnic Culture Research Institute of the Academy of Social Sciences and The National Press Foundation office jointed efforts and organized an investigation group of over 100 people to start collecting information on the Legend of King Gesar performed in all places. Through more than ten years' work, they have collected enough data and published a most complete King Gesar Epic of 120 books, 1 million lines and 20 million words. This is the longest epic in the world.

阿达在那曲赛马会上说唱《格萨尔王传》，数千听众将这里围得水泄不通，大大小小的录音机排成一排 20世纪90年代

Narrator Ada narrating the *Epic of King Gesar* on Nagqu Jockey Meeting. He was surrounded by thousands of audience with large and small recorders lined up in a row in the 1990s.

格萨尔长诗我来讲，	*Poems of Gesar I read,*
王的故事我来说短长。	*The stories of the king I tell.*
轻快的曲调下，	*With lively music,*
国王的征战，多英豪！	*The king's expeditionary wars, how heroic!*
英雄的故事中，	*The hero's stories*
百万奴隶的白骨闪闪，	*Full of white bones of millions of slaves,*
百万母亲的泪汪汪。	*Filled with tears of millions of mothers.*

来听，来赏，
我们歌，我们唱。
歌唱藏人的英雄，
赞我们的格萨尔王。
唱他上马杀敌，
威震四方。
歌他下马抚藏，
爱民慈祥。
又谁知，
开罪了官厅，
斥我们只知“死王”，
不敬“活王”。
笑我们只颂遗者，
不颂当下神王。
我们被赶出茶楼串街坊，
成了下等丐帮。
风里来，雨里唱，
檐下
是我们的唱所，
墙角
是我们的睡房。
嘶哑卖唱伴西风，
饥寒交迫何惨状。
叫天不应，
叫地不灵。
到如今
换天换地换云裳，
脱去丐装进大堂。
歌不尽的英雄大王格萨尔，
数不尽的鲜花何处不放。

Come and listen,
To our melody and our song.
We sing a Tibetan hero,
Our King Gesar to us he belonged.
We sing for his bravery,
We sing for his love of his people along.
But authorities blamed us for singing a dead king,
Instead of a "living king" so strong.
So we were driven out of halls into streets,
And became aboard travelling from town to town.
Walking in winds and singing in rains,
Performing under a roof or in the open ground,
And sleeping in the corner of the wall of the crown.
Today, changes happen under the same sky and earth,
We have proudly entered the grand hall.
Still singing our heroic King Gesar,
We received bouquets of flower everywhere.

四品官车仁·晋美松赞旺布在拍电影 1958年

Tibetan Officer Jigme Songtsen Wangpo filming in 1958.

一个老爷照相，
我们来观赏。
如今轮到我们来拍照，
大家都一样。

A noble lord is taking pictures,
And we are coming and watching that.
Now our turn to take pictures,
And all people are equal.

摄影 *Photography*

Long ago,
There were only three cameras in Tibet.
Belonged to Kalön Ngapoi Ngawang Jigme,
Belonged to Demo Living Buddha,
Belonged to Dalai Lama.
They were treated as magic,
Capturing souls into pictures.
Nowadays,
Not three but thousands of cameras.
Belongs to photographers,
Belongs to families.
Capturing lifestyle,
Into daily life.
New age comes to snowland,
New culture well developed.

拉萨贵族把玩相机 1939年
Lhasa nobles playing with a camera in 1939.

从前
全藏有相机的仅三家：
噶伦阿沛，
德木活佛，
达赖喇嘛。
被认为是高级魔法，
收魂入画。
现在
不是三家是万家。
专业团队，
手机数码。
咔咔咔，
机收画。
雪域更新千万变化，
好一个摄影新文化。

举起相机拍摄的僧侣 2016年
A monk shooting pictures with his camera in 2016.

藏山藏水似无涯，	*Tibetan mountains and rivers seem boundless;*
蓝天彩云幅幅画。	*Its blue sky and colorful clouds are picturesque.*
看我众人争留影，	*It intoxicates all enthusiastic photographers;*
笑容绽放美如花。	*Who find it an impossible task to truly reflect its beauty.*

纳木错 2015年 Namtso Lake in 2015.

藏区高山滑雪 2016年 Highland skiing in Tibet in 2016.

Good sport photos are done by snapshot;
Shooting skiing is shooting the second.
These Tibetan photographers are expert,
Despite being late in this field.
They were heroes in topping the peak,
And being ordinary in mountaineering nowadays.
They have kept the exciting moment,
Leaving good memories for us to enjoy.

滑雪摄影一刹那，
千分一秒不得差。
莫嫌藏人玩此晚，
多有行家出藏家。
从前登峰是英雄，
现时普通你我他。
手指一动倩影在，
留待美图后人夸。

绘画 *Painting*

布达拉宫中在毛毯上作画的画师 1938年

A Tibetan painter drawing on the blanket in the Potala Palace in 1938.

罗布林卡收藏的壁画《大昭寺创始记》 1994年

A mural of Norbulingka collection depicting *The Founding Record of the Jokhang Temple* in 1994.

藏文书法 *Tibetan Calligraphy*

藏民有两种写字的方式，一种是用竹笔和墨水，另一种是用刀笔、白垩粉和黑板。图为一个藏族人手执一支树根形状的刀笔 1906年

There used to be two ways for Tibetans to write. One was to use bamboo pen and ink, and the other was to use a knife or chalk on blackboard. In the picture a Tibetan holding a knife in the shape of a tree root in 1906.

2007年后出现的电脑藏文输入法

Tibetan input method appeared on computer after 2007.

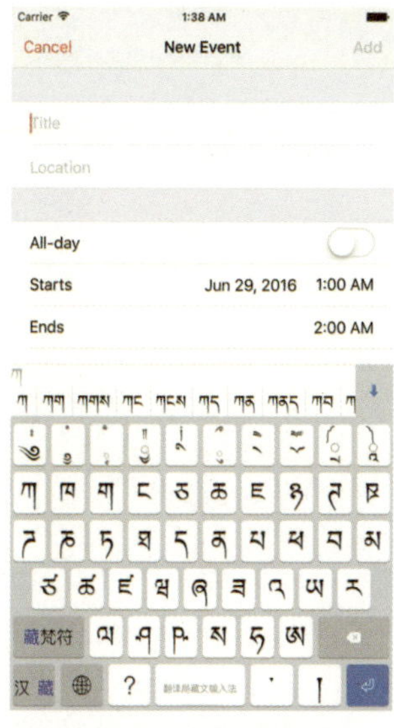

2011年后出现的手机藏文输入法

Tibetan input method appeared on mobile phone after 2011.

登山队编队行军 1960年

The mountaineering team marching in 1960.

To climb up Mount Qomolangma, the world's highest mountain peak, is the goal of mountaineering teams of all countries.

No Chinese had succeeded in climbing up its peak before the 1950s. In 1960, a young Chinese mountaineering team successfully climbed up the peak from the north side.

Mountaineering has been a popular sport among people in Tibet. Hundreds of young Tibetan make team to conquer snow mountains every year. They are active in the snowy mountains, forming a beautiful scenery.

勇登世界高峰，特别是珠穆朗玛峰，是各国登山队员奋勇争先的目标。

20世纪50年代前没有任何中国人成功登顶。1960年，年轻的中国登山队从北坡成功登顶。

在西藏，民众登山已成为民间运动的一大特色。每到登顶季节，总有百人计的藏族青年组成的登山队伍，活跃于雪原之间，形成一道道美丽夺目的风景线。

Set off on the snowy mountain in winter,
Heading to Mount Qomolangma the highest.
Striving forward to find a way in the boundless whiteness,
The tougher it gets, the braver we are.
Snowland surround us,
We decorated snowland.
Does it swallow us,
Or we conquer it?
Neither way,
Because we are completing each other.

冬日出发进雪山，
指向珠峰拉开弦。
茫茫皑皑何是路，
越是艰难越向前。
雪原人海，
人行雪原。
是雪在吞没人，
还是人在划破雪原？
人雪相融，
亲近自然。

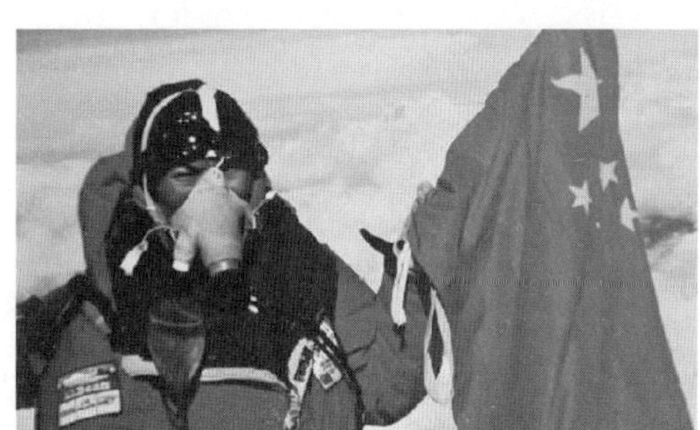

两次登顶珠峰的女登山队员桂桑 20世纪90年代

Kuesang, female member of China Tibet Mountaineering Team, successfully reaching the peak of Mount Qomolangma twice in the 1990s.

藏族登山英雄贡布 1960年

Tibetan mountaineering hero Gongbu in 1960.

我从北坡登顶峰，
跌破眼镜举世穷，
中华健儿一身胆，
踢开艰险任自由。

Success in climbing up the peak from the north side,
Amazes people of the world.
The mountaineering team is brave,
Through tough journey the freedom is in hold.

西藏登山探险队首次登顶卓奥友峰 1985年

China Tibet Mountaineering Team reached the peak of Mount Cho Oyu for the first time in 1985.

Standing on the peak,
We see the blue sky under our feet.
All peaks are in our sight,
Infinite world becomes close for us to meet.

成功登顶脚下天，
举世高峰尽一览。
抬手高呼我来也，
无极世界变有限。

运动会从无到有 *Sports Event, From None to Many*

西藏定日中学运动会的百米赛跑中，学生们冲出起跑线瞬间 2006年

Students rushing out of the starting line during the 100-meter race at the Tingri School sports meeting in 2006.

从1959年实行民主改革以来，西藏本区每年都在传统节日里组织300多次民族传统体育比赛，参加者达4万余人次，观众超过300万人次。西藏体委已挖掘和整理出20多种民族传统体育项目，并努力使这些项目日趋规范化和科学化。

Since the implementation of democratic reform in 1959, Tibet has organized more than 300 ethnic traditional sports competitions each year during traditional festivals. There have been more than 40,000 participants and more than 3 million spectators. The Tibet Sports Commission has discovered and organized more than 20 ethnic and traditional sports programs, and has striven to make these projects increasingly standardized and scientific.

骑马射箭中靶 1956年 Hitting the target on horseback in 1956.

赛马会 2015年 Horse racing event in 2015.

沐浴成日常，
游泳为运动。
散体总归小。
团结才力雄。
不进则退是真言，
不浮即沉是天条。

沐浴节 1956年 Bathing Festival in 1956.

Bathing became a norm,

Swimming became a sport.

Individual is small,

Unity has great power.

Not moving forward means moving backward.

Not to float means to sink.

西藏游泳比赛 2016年 Tibet swimming competition in 2016.

西藏体育运动学校 1999年 Tibet Sports School in 1999.

拉萨市特殊学校的学生们迎来了搬到新校址后的第一次运动会，孩子们在自己力所能及的运动项目上一展身手 2016年 The students of a special school in Lhasa welcomed the first sports event after moving to the new campus. The children showing their skills in their own sports in 2016.

第十一章

除却西藏不是蓝

Chapter 11 Nowhere but Tibet is Always Blue

藏汉一家亲

不要龙王要农王

净天

天地之间

The Friendship of the Han and Tibetan

King of Farmland

Purify the Sky

Heaven and Earth

翱翔蓝天的黑颈鹤 2012年 Black-necked cranes in the sky in 2012.

日东草原上的牧童与小牛犊 1956年 A shepherd boy and his calf on the Ritung Grassland in 1956.

村舍群兽光临，
屋外黑颈鹤叩门。
大自然本一家，
众生灵越走越近。

Wild animals are visiting village houses;
Black-necked cranes are knocking on the door.
In nature we are of one family;
Closer to one another all lives are together.

为了保证藏北地区沿线生态环境，青藏铁路修筑了长度超过160千米、占全长7%的高架桥，桥上供火车行驶，桥下供野生动物迁徙，2010年

In order to ensure the ecological environment along the northern part of Tibet, the Qinghai-Tibet Railway constructed a viaduct over 160 kilometers in length and 7% of the total length. The bridge was especially built for railways to avoid disturbing wildlife migration in 2010.

Riding on horseback day and night,
Bridge piers are like forests and roads high above.
The land for all animals to live,
Harmonious world's beautiful nature.

骑巡千里看夕烟，
桥墩如林路高悬。
留下沃野育百兽，
和谐世界美自然。

一只小藏羚羊与可可西里国家级自然保护区管理局的藏族保护队员索南“亲密接触” 2009年

A Tibetan antelope kissing Sonan, a Tibetan team member of the Kekexili National Nature Reserve Administration in 2009 .

我们同在一个地球村，
我们就是一家人。
来！
走近一步，
我在这边等。
好！
再近一步，
给我一个吻。

In one global village we are;
Of one family we are.
Come on!
Closer,
I am waiting here.
Wonderful!
Even closer,
Give me a kiss.

迁徙的藏羚羊 2012年 Migrating Tibetan antelopes in 2012.

藏羚羊头数翻了二十翻，	*Tibetan antelopes increased by 20 times,*
二十年间从一万到二十万。	*From 10 thousand to 200 thousand in 20 years.*
为什么？	*How come?*
只因有了保护圈，	*Thanks to the protection zones,*
有人在守望，	*Some guarding,*
有人持枪看。	*Some watching with guns.*
冬雪送饲料，	*Supplying foods in snowy winters,*
伤病送诊院。	*The injured sent to the vet hospitals.*
藏羚羊，	*Tibetan antelopes,*
我们相爱在雪原。	*We love each other on the snowy land.*

新年酥油灯节 1938年

Celebrating Butter Lantern Festival in 1938.

到2014年，政府已向拉萨居民免费提供了10万台太阳灶。

By the year 2014, the local government had provided 100,000 free solar stoves to the residents in Lhasa.

哲蚌寺的太阳能路灯 2009年

Solar street lights of Drepung Monastery in 2009.

用太阳灶烧水的藏族老阿妈 2009年

A Tibetan old granny boiling water with solar cooker in 2009.

给农奴主背柴火的农奴 20世纪50年代初 Serfs carrying firewood for their master in the early 1950s.

The "Purify the Sky" program includes forbidding burning yak dung and firewood for cooking, burning pine trees (pinus tabulaeformis) for lighting, and substituting them with gas, solar energy, wind energy and hydro power. Millions of butter lamps have been changed into electric lamps and showers is now using solar energy. Since 2007, plastic bags have been prohibited, 7 years earlier than that of San Francisco in the USA. In addition, electric cables and wires have been buried underground.

净天，包括做饭禁用牛粪和柴火，照明禁用油松，代之以天然气、太阳能、风力发电和水力发电；寺院数百万酥油灯改为电灯；烧水改用太阳能；购物禁用塑料袋（又称“禁白”，实施于2007年，比美国旧金山于2014年实施“禁白”早7年）；电网电缆地下埋。

采用风力发电的寺院 2013年 Temples using wind power in Tibet in 2013.

不要龙王要农王

曲水河谷 20世纪70年代

Chushur Valley in the 1970s.

曲水河谷从天看，
火烧大地黄一片。
今已使，
沃绿青原。

因我得力，
因你有助。
河神也怕你和我，
魔鬼躲上天。

King of Farmland

Looking from the sky at Chushur Valley,
Set on fire, all yellow.
Today all changed,
Green banks and prairie.

Because of my work,
Because of your help.
The river god scared of you and me,
Devils escape to the sky.

曲水河谷 1999年

Chushur Valley in 1999.

曲水河谷 20世纪40年代 Chushur Valley in the 1940s.

曲水

金秋黄昏，
梦乡水畔。
君记否？
那一年，
洪水泛，梁倒田淹到天边，
尸卧田园野狗窜。

如今碧空水蓝，
天上人间。

Chushur

At dusk in golden autumn,
At wonderful riversides.
Do you remember?
At that time,
Due to the floods,
Sorghums fell to water,
Dead bodies everywhere and strayed dogs all over.

Blue sky and blue water at present,
In Heaven and on earth.

曲水两岸的公路和树林 2007年 Highway with trees on both sides of Chushur in 2007.

淹

1940年，
河水淹到布达拉宫山下，
龙王不认神王。
苦了多少百姓，
贵人高处无恙。

大众筑堤挡龙王，
有人又抱佛脚又烧香。
千家万户笑，
笑得天开云畅水顺流，
龙王只得迁宫印度洋。

拉萨河水泛滥 1940年 Kyichu River flooding in 1940.

Floods

In 1940,
To the foot of the Potala mountain, coming the floods,
The Dragon King didn't acknowledg the God King.
Sufferings to the common people,
Joys to the rich and nobles watched on the higher land.

People built dikes to block flood the power of the Dragon King,
Some holding to the Buddha's leg in praying.
People all laughed and smiled,
Smiling the sky open and clouds dispersed and water flowing,
The Dragon King had to leave his palace and move to the Indian Ocean.

布达拉宫上空的吉祥龙云 2015年 Auspicious clouds like a dragon over the Potala Palace in 2015.

拉萨市民齐心协力修筑河堤 20世纪50年代末

Lhasa residents making concerted efforts to build river banks in the late 1950s.

筑起堤岸，
修起路，栽上树。
河水顺流，
地也顺溜。
我们，就是神，
谁敢拦！

拉萨近郊的大棚种植 2007年

Greenhouse cultivation in the suburbs of Lhasa in 2007.

Dikes set up,
Roads built, trees planted.
Smooth flow of the river water,
Pleasing sight of landscape.
We are the gods,
Who dare to stop us!

贺新郎·林芝田园　*The Idyll of Nyingchi*

瘠地林芝卷，	*A painting scroll of Nyingchi County*
满视野，	*Eyeful with,*
田野无边，	*Boundless fields,*
初黄尽染。	*A scene of yellow.*
不是苏杭胜似苏杭，	*Regions south of the Yangtze River are not Suzhou and Hangzhou, but much better,*
江南不再独艳。	*Not the only beautiful place in Southern China.*
一幅画，	*A painting,*
半壁雪原。	*Half of the snow country.*
雅水洗涤现翠微，	*Gentle green from the Yarlung Zangbo River,*
心波起，	*Waves of hearty feelings,*
潮涌情万千。	*Waves of emotional excitement.*
夏殷矣，	*With the summer gone,*
秋实前。	*Comes the harvesting autumn.*
指点江山力换颜。	*Getting the scene to change its look.*
全赖得，	*All relies on,*
你我合缘，	*Your and my*
岁月挥汗。	*Sweaty hard work.*
待到全藏皆绿遍，	*Till Tibet turning all green and,*
映蓝晴空一片。	*The sky all blue.*
唯那时，	*Only then,*
赤心雪苑，	*Chanting with great joy and,*
七彩缤纷拱西藏！	*High aspirations!*
红绿蓝，	*Red, blue and green,*
相拥永长天。	*Embraced in eternity.*
天奈何，	*The heavenly god is hopeless at it,*
情愫展。	*All whole-heartedly satisfied.*

林芝鲁朗田野 1962年 Fields of Lulang, Nyingchi in 1962.

林芝的苹果红了，青稞熟了 20世纪70年代 Harvest of apple and Tibetan barley in Nyingchi in the 1970s.

除却西藏不是蓝，
蓝在爱心映在天。
宇梦萦，宙魂绕，
喜山雅水唤虔诚。

神山冈仁波齐与圣湖玛旁雍错 2016年
Mount Kailash, the sacred mountain and Lake Manasarovar, the holy lake in 2016.

Nowhere but Tibet is always blue,
Calm in people's heart and reflected in the sky.
Dreams of the space, souls of the time,
The Himalayas and the Yarlung Zangpo River calling for piety.

除却西藏不是蓝，
蓝，
映你，
映我。
映你如诗如画，
映我如画如歌。

唯独西藏天最蓝，
蓝，
有你，
有我。
有你长为水，
有我重浴火。

Nowhere but Tibet is always blue,
Blue shines on you,
Also illuminates me.
You're like poetic paintings;
I am like songs of painting.

Only in Tibet is the most blue of blue,
Blue with your offerings,
Also with my offerings.
With you being like water,
I have more fire in the reborn.

念青唐古拉山 2012年 Nyenchen Tanglha Mountains in 2012.

汉藏一家亲

The Friendship of the Han and Tibetan

汉藏合影 2010年

A group of Han and Tibetan taking picture together in 2010.

汉在昆仑东，
藏在昆仑西。
冬同雪原春同水，
片雪滴水心相惜。
心相惜，
情相系，
牵手已度千秋月，
再谱天下大同曲。

Around Kunlun Mountain,
Han is on the east and Tibet on the west.
They share the plateau and drink from the same river,
In autumn, winter, spring, and summer.
Heart close,
They cherish each other.
Hand in hand they have sent away a thousand autumn moons,
And now continue the unity together.

拉萨不远，	*Lhasa is not far,*
心诚在脚前。	*Piety brings it close.*
大昭光近，	*Jokhang light shines,*
一摇到佛缘。	*On prayer-wheels to Lhasa.*
爱心交织处，	*From heart to heart,*
一胞有藏汉。	*One family as we are.*

汉藏紧握手 2016年 Han and Tibetan handshaking in 2016.

同在一棵大树下，	*The wind is mild and the sun is warm,*
风和阳暖好地方。	*Sitting under the same tree in a comfortable form,*
交心座谈尽释怀，	*Chatting with opened hearts and relaxed feeling,*
握手一笑泯怨肠。	*They shake hands with a smile and the tough stops hurting.*

汉人藏人几千年来相依共存，既争又和，既情又缘，却始终以和为主。岁岁年年的你来我往，北京拉萨间再高的山峦也踏出一条大路来。

你看：世上多个民族，谁如汉藏亲近？

东方大地上的汉藏民族偏重于“内向”，所以能共享大乘佛教，主张克制私欲，不是全部以物质来衡量人生，而偏重于内心的富足平和。这就是每年一千多万汉人拥往西藏的潜在意识之源。

明摆着，汉人去藏如此热情的主因，是心之所往，情之所趋，朝亲拜戚，既拜同一大乘佛教在高原的佛地圣寺，也拜同一先祖在雪域开拓的水水山山。

For thousands of years, Hans and Tibetans have been living in coexistence. The Tibetan-Han relation has been both conflicting and harmonious, but the main tone is harmony. Year after year, they communicate and visit each other, treading under their feet a wide road through mountains and rivers between Beijing and Lhasa.

You see: which two nations are as close as Tibetan and Han among so many nations around the world?

In the east, the Tibetans and Hans share Mahayana Buddhism, for they both pay attention to self-cultivation and practice restraining selfish desires. They do not aim their life goal with material gains but inner peace and abundance. This is the hidden consciousness behind the reason why Tibet attracts more than 10 million Han people going for visit and pilgrimage each year.

Obviously, the main reasons of the Han people going to visit Tibet so enthusiastically are following their hearts and feelings, visiting their kith and kin, pilgrimage the Buddha-stage and the Holy temples of the same Mahayana Buddhism on the plateau as well as the mountains and rivers exploited in the snowland by the same ancestors.

认藏亲，
认汉亲。
万水千山不觉远，
一脉中华情。
看笑脸，
看嘴圆。
左也像来右也像，
谁说不是一家人？

We search for Tibetan relatives,
We search for Han relatives,
Thousands of miles doesn't feel far.
One blood line shared by all Chinese.
The smiling faces,
The smiling mouths,
You look like me, and I look like you.
Who would say we are not from the same family of one nation?

藏族男孩与汉族男孩 2011年 Tibetan boy and Han boy in 2011.

我的血里有你的因，
我的命里有你的根。
走遍中原到雪原，
一水一山只为寻。
寻啊，寻，
到如今。
行啊，行，
几曾停。
蓝天云外不觉远，
脚下咫尺近。
不待铁鞋踏破时，
圆梦一个情。

I have your gene in my blood;
You have roots in my life.
From the Central Plains to the snowy highland,
Crossing rivers and mountains I try to find.
Repeated walking;
Repeated searching.
Even if it is to the blue sky and white cloud in distance,
I find it not far for it has significance.
Socks worn and shoes worn, I still marching to my destination,
Till my dream has come true, just for my affection.

后记 / 虔诚如诗，昭心若歌

2017年深秋，91岁的爷爷在美国走了，带着对亲人的思念、对祖国的牵挂、对雪域高原的眷恋与遗憾走了。

爷爷的一生与西藏这片圣地，结下了深深的情缘。由于工作、学术和情有独钟的原因，从20世纪50年代第一次随军进西藏始，爷爷先后八次进藏。年富力强时去，年逾古稀之后还去，有六次进藏是在他75岁之后，而最后一次进藏已是80多岁高龄。每一次西藏之行，都在他人生的不同阶段留下了不一样的烙印，都让他经历了独特的心灵洗礼。

当他在青年时代跋涉入藏，历经艰险后突见雪域高原那纯净透彻的天地时，他感到心胸洞开、心驰神往；当他在壮年时虔诚回藏，那些雄伟庄严的寺庙、天籁般的藏族歌声、巧夺天工的艺术品、虔诚礼佛的藏民，让他如醉如痴，感到人与神可以离得那么近；当他在暮年时像感到了召唤般屡屡入藏，在熟悉又陌生的地方遇见一个个一群群质朴虔诚、友善勤劳的藏族同胞，他一次次体味到藏汉一家亲的温暖。爷爷无数次感慨："不到雪域不知爱，除却西藏不是蓝。"

爷爷一次次入藏，每一次都亲眼看到那里新的变化。他喜欢摄影，用相机记录了一个个地方的日新月异，一个个家庭、一张张笑脸饱含的苦辣酸甜。在雪域圣地，沧桑男女千百里风餐露宿磕长头朝圣，白发老人一刻不停地转动经筒，少男少女经不离口……他们祈求幸福，向往天堂。爷爷常对我们说：藏胞礼佛的那份虔诚，举世仅有，虔诚如诗！但是，改变他们命运的不是神，而是人，是他们自己的汗水和中华民族一家亲的手足之情。

爷爷移居美国后，不时听到有人对西藏说三道四，说什么西藏残破不堪、民不聊生、文化凋敝、宗教信仰不自由等；每当这种时候，他火冒三丈、义愤填膺！他四处向人介绍自己在西藏的所见所闻，撰文驳斥一些人对西藏的攻击，通过媒体与"藏独"人士辩论。在此期间，他深入研究了西藏历史，这些又促使他在晚年多次入藏，亲自感受、拍摄西藏的新面貌。

在完成并于美国成功出版了揭露南京大屠杀和细菌战的书后，爷爷于古稀之年开始整理自己在西藏拍摄的照片，收集有关资料，撰写诗歌，创作了《虔诚如诗》一书并在美国出版。该书出版后，产生了较大的影响。在新书发布会上，达赖的追随者出面刁难。爷爷义正词严地说："你只要指出书中有一幅照片是假的，我服输愿罚。我书中的照片有假的吗？"达赖的追随者哑口无言。爷爷更将自己多年的研究成果展示出来，指出了"藏独"人士发表的有关西藏的虚假照片、虚假文字等。

后来，为了进一步反映西藏在文化方面的进步，近90岁高龄的爷爷又在美国创作出版了《昭心如歌》。

爷爷一直有一个心愿：在自己的祖国出版一本反映西藏变化的书。一者为祖国献上一份海外赤子爱祖国、爱西藏的心意；再者现在不少人更信外国人说的话，那就让他们听听他这个美籍华人的见闻和感悟吧。在许多热心人的帮助下，爷爷终于如愿以偿，他创作的《雪域圣地的前世今生——我眼中的西藏60年》由天地出版社出版了。本书图文并茂，书中的照片，一部分是爷爷一次次进藏亲手拍摄，一部分来自他多年来的收集和整理。爷爷只是一个摄影爱好者，拍的照片谈不上多少艺术性，但的的确确是对真情实景的记录。书中的文字是他写的诗。本书将西藏的前世与今生以照片的形式对比呈现，以诗歌的形式直抒胸臆。

爷爷谈不上有多高的文学素养，写的诗多似白话，但真真切切是他心底深情的流露。爷爷常说：关于西藏，我不管别人说什么，我只说自己的亲眼所见，只抒发我的主观情感，看到的人自然会懂。爷爷的诗，在我眼里是那么的拙趣真切、赤诚如歌。

为了本书的出版，爷爷不顾高龄几次回国与大家一起讨论书稿，协商有关事宜。病重之际，他还在关心本书的出版进展情况。遗憾的是，爷爷没有看到这本精美的书；庆幸的是，他的愿望已经圆满实现了。

在本书出版之际，我代表我爷爷、我父亲，感谢四川新华发行集团的朱丹枫董事长、新华文轩出版传媒股份有限公司原总编辑张京，以及四川省新闻出版局的有关同志，没有他们的关心和支持，就没有本书的出版；感谢经典记忆文化传播公司的邹小工、张迪和天地出版社的同志，没有他们艰苦细致的工作，就没有本书现在的面貌。谢谢了，所有为爷爷圆梦的亲人和朋友！

愿更多的人通过这本书了解西藏、热爱西藏。

愿本书化作一炷心香，告慰爷爷在天英灵！

尹家琤
2018年夏

PREFACE / Poetic Devoutness, Cantabile Royalty

In fall, 2017 my 91-year-old grandfather left the world at his home in the USA with his love for family and homeland China along with his unfinished dream for Tibet.

Grandfather developed deep love and remarkable fate with Tibet during his lifetime. He went to Tibet for 8 times, ever since the very first time he stepped on the land of Tibet with army in the 1950s. 6 of these visits were made after his age of 75. He took the final trip to Tibet when he was over 80. Every trip marked an era and made a spiritual baptism in his life.

When grandfather visited Tibet in his youth he was amazed by such unique landscape and pure nature gifts after such a suffering trip on horse through mountains with mud paths; when he visited Tibet in his midlife he developed deep devoutness after witnessing those majestic lama temples, royalty of people, remarkable holy songs and folk arts; when he went to Tibet for several times as if he was beckoned during the twilight of his life, he was deeply moved by the kindness and simpleness of Tibetans with their enthusiastic love for Han nationality. He wondered for many times that how love can be as pure as snow mountain and how kindness can be as beautiful as blue sky in Tibet.

Grandfather witnessed different eras and many changes of Tibet over times. By his photography he captured many developing places, characteristic families and bitter and sweet faces. In this holy snow land men and women lean for kowtowing pilgrimage through all the vicissitudes of bitter journey; children chant scriptures while elderly people turn their prayer wheels every day to pray for happiness and heaven. My grandfather often told me how rare the Tibetans' devoutness was that it was so poetic to feel but he knew that it wasn't god who turned their destiny but themselves with their hardwork and help from the love of Han Chinese.

After grandfather moved to the USA he frequently heard scandals and extreme opinions about Tibet, complaining undeveloped environment, poverty, lack of culture and faith and so on. Irritated yet encouraged grandfather then started to share his experiences in Tibet by writing articles to refute false report, debating on TV and radio with Tibetan Separatists while investigated many historic, cultural and religious facts of Tibet throughout years. All of these works encouraged him to make many trips to Tibet during his elderly age.

After completing the books of *The Rape of Nanking* and *The Rape of Biological Warfare*, grandfather started to focus on documenting photos he took and facts he saw in Tibet, writing poems and finally produced the book *Poetic Devoutness* which was published in the USA. The book made a major influence at the time. On the day of new book launch Dalai's followers challenged grandfather, with confidence and pride grandfather said: I will give up defeat if you can point out any fake photo in my book, can you do that? The challenger from Dalai group was then in silence.

Grandfather even showed more true pictures he took along with his investigation of how Tibetan Separatists published fake photos and articles. After the success of *Poetic Devoutness* grandfather continued his work and published the second book of the Tibet series in the USA named *Spiritual Heart Song* despite his health condition at the age of 90.

Grandfather had a longed-for dream that is to publish a book in his beloved native country about the old and new Tibet. He was eager to share his passion as well as true stories and memories with his own prospect as a Chinese living in the USA. Under many helping hands his dream now has a chance to come true. Tiandi Press is publishing this book of *The Past 60 Years and Present of Tibet in My Eyes*. The book presents and compares true pictures of Tibet in old and new age, many of them were taken by my grandfather and the rest of them were selected by him. Grandfather wasn't a professional photographer or poet, but his photos and words are true and sincere. I used to hear from him for many times saying that no matter what people said he alway believed his own eyes and wished to share his own experience and emotion, people would understand from these pictures and poems without no more explanations. Anyhow, to me his poems are so pure and sincere that make them adorable enough to read and understand his meaningful sharing.

However, while my father and I are so grateful that now my grandfather's dream came true, we feel it a pity that grandfather has no chance to witness this book's publication. Grandfather used to fly back to China for many times to discuss publishing matters about the book with Tiandi Press, and he cared deeply for the publishing progress even during his final days in serious illness. In the names of my father and grandfather I now would like to thank Mr. Zhu Danfeng, the Chairman of the Xinhua Winshare Publishing and Media Co., Ltd., Mr. Zhang Jing, the former Chief Editor of Xinhua Winshare Publishing and Media Co., Ltd. and many people from Press and Publication Bureau of Sichuan, for their major contribution in publishing this book. My sincere appreciation is also from the hard works of Mrs. Zou Xiaogong, Mr. Zhang Di from Classic Memory Cultural Communication Co., Ltd. and many people from Tiandi Press as they made this book so decent.

I wish that there will be more people willing to get to know and eventually love Tibet from reading this book.

May this book become a incense from my heart to bless grandfather in heaven.

Yin Jiacheng,

Summer 2018

图片摄影 PHOTOGRAPHY

（排名不分先后） (In no particular order)

尹集钧	James Yin
全绍清	Quan Shaoqing
曾承东	Zeng Chengdong
陈宗烈	Chen Zonglie
德木活佛	Demo Living Buddha
德木旺久多吉	Demo Waju Dorje
金　勇	Jin Yong
庄学本	Zhuang Xueben
蓝志贵	Lan Zhigui
李仲魁	Li Zhongkui
吕玲珑	Lv Linglong
张仁华	Zhang Renhua
王春蓉	Wang Chunrong
秦　璇	Qin Xuan
侯德强	Hou Deqiang
汪成建	Wang Chengjian
觉　果	Jueguo
普布扎西	Pubo Tashi
格桑达瓦	Kesang Dawa
郭绪雷	Guo Xulei
张汝锋	Zhang Rufeng
刘　坤	Liu Kun
恩斯特·塞弗尔（德）	Ernst Schäfer (German)
奥夫舍·诺尔祖诺夫（俄）	Ovshe Norzunov (Russian)
哈利·斯陶顿（英）	Harry Staunton (British)
查尔斯·贝尔（英）	Charles A. Bell (British)
弗雷德里克·查普曼（英）	Fredrick Chapman (British)
黎吉生（英）	Hugh Richardson (British)
绕登·雷布查（印度）	Rabden Lepcha (Indian)
帕塞瓦尔·兰登（英）	Perceval Landon (British)
《西藏历史图志》	*A Picture Album of the History of Tibet*

拉萨河大桥 2014年 Kyichu River Bridge in 2014.

Some of the images used in this book have been collected by James Yin for many years. Editors and publishers have paid to the right holders of the pictures used in this book in various ways, but we are still unable to get in touch with some authors. We sincerely thank every author and apologize to those whom we have not yet contacted. We hope the right holders of the pictures in this book can contact us in time so that we can pay the remuneration. Please contact tianditg@163.com.

本书使用的部分图片系作者多年收集整理而来。编者和出版社已通过各种途径向本书中所使用的图片权利人支付稿酬，但仍有部分作者无法取得联系。我们真诚感谢每一位作者，从尊重作者权益出发，我们对尚未取得联系的权利人表示深深的歉意。我们希望得知本书出版的权利人及时与我们联系，以便我们奉上稿酬。

联系方式：tianditg@163.com

图书在版编目（CIP）数据

雪域圣地的前世今生：我眼中的西藏60年 / ［美］尹集钧编著. ——成都：天地出版社, 2019.12
ISBN 978-7-5455-5259-1

Ⅰ. ①雪… Ⅱ. ①尹… Ⅲ. ①西藏—地方史 Ⅳ. ①K297.5

中国版本图书馆CIP数据核字(2019)第236862号

XUEYU SHENGDI DE QIANSHIJINSHENG: WO YANZHONG DE XIZANG 60 NIAN

雪域圣地的前世今生：我眼中的西藏60年

出品人　杨　政
编　著　尹集钧
责任编辑　田　曦　李　倩
封面设计　尹家琤
版式设计　经典记忆文化传播有限公司
责任印刷　刘　元

出版发行　天地出版社
（成都市槐树街2号　邮政编码：610014）
（北京市方庄芳群园3区3号　邮政编码：100078）
网　址　http://www.tiandiph.com
电子邮箱　tianditg@163.com
经　销　新华文轩出版传媒股份有限公司

印　刷　天津画中画印刷有限公司
版　次　2019年12月第一版
印　次　2019年12月第一次印刷
成品尺寸　210mm × 280mm　1/16
印　张　18.5
字　数　300千
定　价　88.00元
书　号　ISBN 978-7-5455-5259-1

咨询电话：（028）87734639（总编室）
购书热线：（010）67693207（营销中心）